WESSEX

God will towards men

WESSEX

Text by Robin Whiteman
Photography by Rob Talbot

TED SMART

The right of Robin Whiteman and Rob Talbot to be identified as authors of this work
has been asserted by them in accordance with the Copyright, Designs and Patents Act 1988.

First published in Great Britain in 1994 by George Weidenfeld and Nicolson Ltd
The Orion Publishing Group, Orion House, 5 Upper St Martin's Lane, London WC2H 9EA

This edition produced for The Book People Ltd
Guardian House, Borough Road, Goldalming, Surrey GU7 2AE

Designed by Paul Ryan
Map by Bob Monks
Printed and bound in Italy

British Library Cataloguing-in-Publication Data
A catalogue record for this book is available from the British Library.

ISBN 297 83260 3

Front cover: Gold Hill, Shaftesbury, Dorset. Overlooking the Vale of Blackmoor, the thatched and tiled stone cottages of the village are dominated by the massive buttressed precinct wall of the former abbey founded in *c.* 888 by Alfred the Great for Benedictine nuns.

Half-title page: Angel in the church of St Peter and St Paul at Muchelney, Somerset

Title Page: Axbridge, Dorset. Once an important Anglo-Saxon town, fortified stronghold and borough with a royal mint, Axbridge developed into a prosperous medieval wool centre specializing in knitted stockings. In the market square,

the timber-framed King John's Hunting Lodge (at left) belonged to a prosperous merchant around 1500 and is now owned by the National Trust. Facing the Lamb Inn is the carved and painted head of King John, which was originally a pub sign.

Back cover: Old Harry Rocks, Studland, Dorset. The Old Harry Rocks were once part of a chalk ridge that linked Dorset with the Isle of Wight. Old Harry (namely the Devil) is the single pinnacle furthest away from the headland.

Contents

Acknowledgements

Robin Whiteman and Rob Talbot would particularly like to acknowledge the generous co-operation of English Heritage (Historic Properties South-West and Historic Properties South-East) and the two National Trust Regional Offices of Wessex and Southern for allowing them to take photographs of their properties and sites featured in this book. Additional thanks go to Diana Lanham, Manager of the National Trust Photographic Library. They are also extremely grateful to Lisa and Mark Roper of Forde Abbey; Lionel Green, owner of Compton Acres; and Lionel Smart, owner of Stanton Drew Stone Circles. Special thanks go to Judith Dooling. Appreciation also goes to all those individuals and organizations too numerous to mention by name who have nevertheless made valuable contributions. Grateful thanks go to Colin Grant, our editor at Weidenfeld and Nicolson for so many years, and a warm welcome to Lucas Dietrich and Emma Way, who now take on responsibility for the Country Series, as editor and editorial director respectively.

Author's Note

Wessex, for the purpose of this book, covers the counties of Wiltshire, Hampshire, Dorset, Somerset and Avon. However, parts of this region have been included in either *The Cotswolds* or *The West Country* – companion volumes in the Country Series – and have therefore not been repeated. The exception is Bath, which now appears in both *Wessex* and *The Cotswolds*. To be more specific, Wessex includes that part of Somerset east of Barnstaple and Taunton, including the Somerset Levels; all of Dorset; and that part of Wiltshire, Hampshire and Avon south of the M4 motorway. It should be noted that in June 1993 the Local Government Commission recommended that Avon should be abolished, the city of Bristol should return to county status, and Somerset should have its historic boundaries restored.

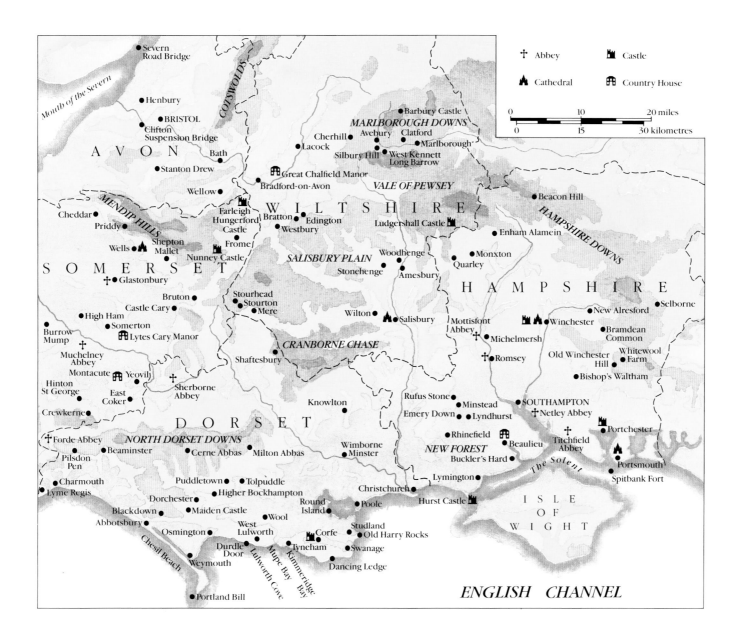

† Abbey   🏰 Castle

🏛 Cathedral   🏠 Country House

0   10   20 miles

0   15   30 kilometres

Severn
Road Bridge

Mouth of the Severn

Henbury

BRISTOL

Clifton
Suspension Bridge

Bath

COTSWOLDS

A V O N

Stanton Drew

Wellow

Barbury Castle

MARLBOROUGH DOWNS

Cherhill   Avebury   Clatford

Lacock   Marlborough

Silbury Hill   West Kennett
Long Barrow

Great Chalfield Manor

Bradford-on-Avon

VALE OF PEWSEY

W I L T S H I R E

Beacon Hill

HAMPSHIRE DOWNS

MENDIP HILLS

Cheddar

Priddy

Wells   Shepton
Mallet

Farleigh
Hungerford
Castle

Bratton   Edington
Westbury

Frome

Nunney Castle

Ludgershall Castle

Enham Alamein

S O M E R S E T

SALISBURY PLAIN

Woodhenge

Stonehenge   Amesbury

Monxton

Quarley

H A M P S H I R E

† Glastonbury

Bruton

Castle Cary

High Ham

Somerton

Burrow
Mump

Lytes Cary Manor

Stourhead
Stourton
Mere

Wilton   🏛 Salisbury

Mottisfont
Abbey

New Alresford   Selborne

🏰🏛 Winchester

Bramdean
Common

Michelmersh

Old Winchester
Hill   Whitewool
Farm

† Muchelney
Abbey

Montacute   Yeovil

Hinton
St George

East
Coker

Sherborne
Abbey

CRANBORNE CHASE

Shaftesbury

† Romsey

Bishop's Waltham

Crewkerne

Knowlton

Rufus Stone

Minstead

Emery Down   Lyndhurst

SOUTHAMPTON

† Netley Abbey

† Forde Abbey

NORTH DORSET DOWNS

Beaminster

Cerne Abbas   Milton Abbas

Wimborne
Minster

NEW FOREST

Buckler's Hard

Rhinefield   🏠 Beaulieu   Titchfield
Abbey

Portchester

Pilsdon
Pen

D O R S E T

Lymington

Portsmouth

The Solent

Spitbank Fort

Charmouth

Lyme Regis

Puddletown   Tolpuddle

Higher Bockhampton

Christchurch

Hurst Castle

I S L E
O F
W I G H T

Dorchester

Blackdown

Maiden Castle

Wool

Round
Island

Poole

Abbotsbury

Osmington

West
Lulworth

Studland
Old Harry Rocks

Chesil Beach

Durdle
Door

Tyneham

Corfe

Swanage

Weymouth

Lulworth Cove

Mupe Bay

*Kimmeridge
Bay*

Dancing Ledge

Portland Bill

E N G L I S H   C H A N N E L

Introduction

GLASTONBURY TOR

Once surrounded by the undrained watery wastes of the Somerset Levels, Glastonbury Tor has long been associated with the Isle of Avalon of Arthurian legend. The supposed discovery of the bones of both Arthur and Guinevere in the grounds of Glastonbury Abbey in 1191 furthered the tradition. Joseph of Arimathea, the first-century missionary, is also said to have settled at Glastonbury, bringing with him the Holy Grail. Having thrust his staff into the ground on Wearyall Hill, it sprouted, hence the origin of the Glastonbury Thorn, which before the adoption of the Gregorian calendar in 1752 bloomed on Christmas Day. An alleged cutting from the original tree can be found in the abbey grounds. The Grail is said to have been buried near the source of the Chalice Well (or Blood Spring) at the foot of the Tor. The iron-red waters have a reputation for healing. The 518-foot-high Tor is topped by the late fourteenth-century tower of St Michael's, all that remains of a church that replaced a chapel destroyed by an earthquake in *c.* 1300.

Hovering hundreds of feet above the undulating downland, a skylark sustains its clear warbling song. On the slopes beneath the grass-covered ramparts of an Iron Age hill-fort, a shining white horse stands petrified in chalk. Amid swollen fields of golden wheat, a perfect circle of flattened corn puzzles the curious and leads to colourful explanations about its origin: from flying saucers to a 'plasma vortex' (a new kind of whirlwind). Running straight between verdant hedgerows, a Roman road points to a cleft on the horizon, where far beyond lies the ancient city of *Aquae Sulis*, with its promise of healing waters and hot mineral springs. Hidden within the folds of the hills, a small convoy of travellers threads its way along a secret lane, drawn by invisible lines of energy emanating from a distant pagan temple. A trout-filled stream emerges into the valley, where the limestone tower of a sacred church dominates a sleepy market town. Sheep graze on the springy turf. A blue adonis flits across the grassland. And a solitary walker follows the old green path that leads into the heart of the sarsen-strewn plain.

The Wessex landscape has, in Thomas Hardy's words, a 'partly real, partly dream' quality. Underlying the visible, more than anywhere else in England, lurks the hint of unseen forces: timeless energies stretching back into the prehistoric past; invisible currents – ley lines – forming spiritual pathways across the country and linking sacred sites. Memories of these ancient forces survive in the traditions and legends of the Wessex people. Stories of giants, devils, witches and ghosts abound, and in more recent times UFOs, or Unidentified Flying Objects, have added to the myths. Not surprisingly, many of the stories of inexplicable phenomena occur within the vicinity of prehistoric temples like Stonehenge, megalithic sanctuaries like those near Avebury, and downland barrows like the Giant's Grave (of which there are several) and the Devil's Den. In a landscape brimming with legends, Glastonbury holds a special fascination. This is the blessed island of Avalon, paradise of Celtic gods, entrance to the underworld, final resting place of the Holy Grail, site of the first Christian church, and burial place of Arthur, the 'Once and Future King'. Also in Somerset, Cadbury Castle clambers for recognition as the site of Arthur's Camelot.

Its legends aside, Wessex offers much that is unique. Certainly, it contains the largest number of prehistoric monuments in Britain. A list of some of its greatest treasures reads like entries in the Guinness Book of Records: the 'Sweet Track', the oldest known road in Britain, possibly in Europe; Avebury, the largest surviving stone circle in Britain; Windmill Hill, site of the earliest Neolithic farming culture in England; Silbury Hill, the largest artificial mound in Europe; and Stonehenge, the most famous stone circle in the world.

The architecture of the region is a celebration of the wide variety of materials. Cotswold oolite limestone predominates in the north-west, particularly in the 'golden city' of Bath and towns like Bradford-on-Avon. In the foothills of the Mendips, Doulting crystalline limestone, from the quarries near Shepton Mallet, can be found in numerous churches, including Glastonbury Abbey and Wells Cathedral. Ham Hill Liassic limestone, from the quarries near Montacute in southern Somerset, prevails in villages like Hinton St George and East Coker, as well as in many of the magnificent church towers for which Somerset is justly famous. Dorset possesses some of the finest building stone in the country: Purbeck marble, several sorts of Jurassic limestones (most notably Portland stone) and stone roofing slates from the Purbeck quarries. Salisbury Cathedral is built of Chilmark stone, similar to that found in the Portland beds. Both Avebury and Stonehenge are constructed of sarsen sandstone, found on the Marlborough Downs. Chalk (an exceptionally pure limestone) covers much of Wessex but is rarely used as a building material. Flint, however, which occurs in the chalk, is often used for walling, either on its own or in combination with another stone. There is also cob (a mixture of chalky mud and straw), which is used in cottages like those at Milton Abbas. Timber framing is especially noticeable in areas like the New Forest, while brick and tiles are often used where the materials for their manufacture are readily available.

Yet, despite the special qualities of the landscape and the wide variety of building materials, despite the wealth of archaeological, historical and industrial sites, it is the people of Wessex – ordinary and famous, past and present – who bring life, colour and drama to the region. Among those who have achieved prominence are people like William Henry Fox Talbot, inventor of the negative-positive photographic process; Isambard Kingdom Brunel, designer of the Clifton Suspension Bridge; Alfred the Great, King of Wessex; the Duke of Monmouth, claimant to the English Crown and leader of the Pitchfork Rebellion; John Cabot, 'discoverer' of Nova Scotia and Newfoundland; and Lord Mountbatten of Broadlands, who was killed while holidaying in Ireland. Less well-known people include: Alexander Keiller, the millionaire responsible for the restoration of prehistoric Avebury; Henry Hoare 'the Magnificent', creator of Stourhead Garden; and the Tolpuddle Martyrs, sentenced to transportation for seven years for administering an illegal oath!

In literary terms Wessex may be undeniably Thomas Hardy's, but there are countless other writers who – even if only in part – have staked some claim to the region: T. E. Lawrence (Lawrence of Arabia), who was killed in a motorcycle accident near Bovington Camp; the American-born T. S. Eliot, whose ancestors came from the village of East Coker; Jane Austen, who was born at Steventon, Hampshire; John Fowles, author of *The French Lieutenant's Woman*; the three Powys brothers of Montacute; Gilbert White, the clergyman responsible for the classic *The Natural History and Antiquities of Selborne*; Richard Adams, author of *Watership Down*; Izaak Walton, angler and biographer who spent his last years at Winchester; William Barnes, the Dorset dialect poet; Charles Dickens, born in a small terraced house in Portsmouth; Richard Jefferies, son of a Wiltshire farmer; Alfred Williams, 'the hammerman poet' and author of *A Wiltshire Village*; George Meredith, the Portsmouth-born novelist and poet; W. H. Hudson, author of *A Shepherd's Life*; Celia Fiennes, born at the manor house in Newton Toney, Wiltshire; and Philip Edward Thomas, the poet who was inspired by the countryside of Steep and Froxfield in East Hampshire.

In *The Description of Britain* (1480) William Caxton called Stonehenge one of the most wonderful of the many wonders in Britain. Other wonders included the great underground cavern at Cheddar, 'hot wells' like those found at Bath, and an unidentified 'hollow in the earth, or cavern,' near Winchester, 'out of which a strong wind always blows, so that no-one can stand outside it for any length of time'. All of these 'marvels and wonders', and possibly more mentioned by Caxton (could they be identified), are in Wessex. Today, five centuries later, others clamour to be added to the list: Stourhead, one of England's finest eighteenth-century landscape gardens, which incorporates the church and village of Stourton into its grand design; the magical landscape of Glastonbury, with its legendary tor and healing springs; the Jurassic rocks of the Dorset coast that contain fossilized creatures from the distant past . . . the marvels and wonders of Wessex are most wonderful indeed.

Avebury and Wiltshire

WEST KENNETT AVENUE AVEBURY

Snaking a curious course from the Sanctuary on Overton Hill to the Avebury Circles – a distance of one-and-a-half miles – the West Kennett Avenue originally had about 100 pairs of stones, many of which were buried in medieval times on the church's orders or removed for building material. By the 1930s, when Alexander Keiller began to rebuild the Neolithic avenue, only four stones were standing, and a further nine were partly visible. Thought to have been used for ceremonial purposes, the avenue was erected in *c.* 2300 BC, a few hundred years after the erection of the main henge and circles. In the eighteenth century William Stukeley speculated on the existence of a second avenue leading west towards the Long Stones, near Beckhampton. Largely reconstructed by Keiller, the Avebury Circles comprise an irregular main circle 1100 feet in diameter that encompasses two smaller circles 330 feet across, the northernmost of which once contained an even smaller circle. The village of Avebury, built out of the broken stones, lies partly within the circles.

At the same time as the boy-king Tutankhamen was buried in his treasure-laden tomb in the Valley of the Kings on the west bank of the Egyptian Nile, the rich and powerful early Bronze Age élite, known as the Wessex Culture, which ruled southern England for about five hundred years, was in decline. Although there was no clear-cut transition from early to middle to late Bronze Age, the mid-fourteenth century BC saw a change in religious customs, an improvement in metallurgical skills and a further shift away from the old hunting-and-gathering lifestyle towards an increasing number of agricultural settlements, particularly on the chalk downland of Wiltshire and Hampshire. The landscape was also changing. Forest clearance was rapidly accelerated with metal tools; permanent villages, composed of groups of circular huts, were being surrounded by field systems and enclosures; cattle, sheep and goats were being encouraged to graze on cleared land to prevent regrowth; valuable weapons and ornaments ceased to be placed in graves; and many of the ancient sites, like Avebury and Stonehenge, were becoming overgrown and neglected.

As years turned to centuries, centuries to millennia, successive waves of immigrants and invaders from continental Europe settled in Wessex. Celts, Romans, Anglo-Saxons and Normans – all left their mark on the landscape: Iron Age hill-forts, Roman villas and roads, Anglo-Saxon monasteries and great linear earthworks, Norman motte-and-bailey castles and magnificent stone cathedrals.

Throughout this time, the great Neolithic henge and its stone circles at Avebury – dating from between about 3710 BC and 2000 BC – stood relatively undisturbed. On its south-western side the Anglo-Saxons established a large settlement, possibly incorporating part of the earthworks into some sort of fortification. The prehistoric site came to be known as 'Waledich', or 'dyke of the Britons'. A church was built just north of the village in the ninth or tenth century. The Normans enlarged the church and in 1114 founded a small Benedictine priory on the site of the present Avebury Manor. It was the close proximity of the church to the pagan 'temple' that led to the destruction of much of prehistoric Avebury. By the end of the twelfth century monks and clerics were determined to rid the landscape, once and for all, of its pre-Christian past. Equipped with iron spades, crowbars and various other tools, groups of workmen set about the enormous task of removing the stones. Deep pits were dug, into which one stone after another was toppled over and completely buried.

It was a dangerous operation, as one unfortunate worker found out: while he was helping to dig one of the pits, a massive stone fell over unexpectedly and crushed him to death. The body lay in the ground, buried with the stone, until 1938, when it was discovered by Alexander Keiller, who had purchased the site and was restoring the ancient monument. From the contents of the man's leather purse it was deduced that he was probably a travelling barber-surgeon, who had been coerced by the church into helping to bury the stones. Silver coins in his possession helped to pinpoint the date of his death to around 1320. Yet, even after being freed from under the stone, the medieval man's bones were dogged by bad luck – almost as if they were cursed. Sent to London for further examination, his remains were destroyed by a bomb in 1941.

Burying the stones, however, helped to preserve them. After the late seventeenth century many of those left standing were broken up for use as local building material. By then the village of Avebury had begun to encroach inside the perimeter of the circle itself. Keiller's excavation and reconstruction of the great henge in the 1930s involved the removal of vast quantities of old agricultural rubbish and the demolition of numerous buildings, including pigsties, a garage and a windmill. Today the partially reconstructed circle is divided roughly into quarters by four roads that meet almost in the centre, near the Red Lion Inn.

Although Avebury may not be quite as famous as Stonehenge, it is more than fourteen times larger, some five hundred years older, and the arrangement of stones has been less disturbed. In fact, of the nine hundred or so circles surviving in Britain, it is the biggest and grandest. Avebury and most of Stonehenge were built of large stones known as sarsens – unworked in the former and shaped in the latter. Scattered throughout the downland around Marlborough, sarsens are the broken remnants of a particularly hard form of sandstone that was laid down over the chalk some twenty to thirty million years ago. The origin of the name 'sarsen' is surrounded by controversy. Some claim that it derived from the word 'Saracen', meaning 'alien' or 'heathen', while others argue that it is derived from the Old English *sar* and *stan*, meaning 'troublesome stone'. Sarsens were also called 'grey wethers' because of their resemblance to sheep grazing on the downland. Those at Avebury vary in size: the largest stands over nineteen feet high and the heaviest weighs over sixty tons.

The greatest concentration of prehistoric monuments, not only in Wessex but in Britain, occurs in Wiltshire. In addition to Avebury and Stonehenge, there are several others that are of great archaeological importance: Silbury Hill, the largest man-made prehistoric mound in Europe; Windmill Hill, site of the earliest Neolithic farming culture in England; the West Kennett Long Barrow, one of the longest Neolithic burial chambers in Britain; and Little Woodbury, south of Salisbury, an Iron Age farmstead originally enclosed within a four-hundred-foot-diameter timber stockade. Other major prehistoric sites in Wessex include Maiden Castle in Dorset, possibly the most famous Iron Age hill-fort in the country; the Iron Age lake village of Glastonbury in Somerset; the Stanton Drew stone circles in the Mendips; and the limestone caves at Cheddar, first occupied by Palaeolithic (Old Stone Age) hunters from as far back as about 30,000 BC.

The Neolithic hill-top enclosure on Windmill Hill, near Avebury – like those on Whitesheet Hill and Knap Hill – is known as a causewayed camp. Roughly circular in plan, these enclosures consist of one or more concentric rings of banks and ditches broken by undug gaps, or causeways, which may have been entrances. Among the carefully buried objects revealed in excavations of the ditches at different sites in southern England were flint scrapers, stone axes, animal bones, human skulls, young children and – at Whitehawk in Sussex – a mother with her new-born child. Although the function of the camps is unclear, it has been variously suggested that they were settlement sites built for defensive purposes, centres for periodic fairs and tribal gatherings, cattle enclosures, or open cemeteries for the exposure of corpses. Nowadays the consensus seems to be that they were probably ritual cult centres where people gathered at certain times of the year to perform ceremonies relating to birth, death and regeneration.

A passion for archaeology led George Edward Stanhope Molyneaux Herbert, 5th Earl of Carnarvon, to the Valley of the Kings in Egypt, where in 1922 he and Howard Carter discovered the tomb of Tutankhamen. Shortly after, Carnarvon was bitten by a mosquito, and within a month he died from blood poisoning. His body was taken back to England, where it was buried on the summit of Beacon Hill, overlooking his family home, Highclere Castle. Intentionally or not, by choosing to be laid to rest on the site of an Iron Age hill-fort, Carnarvon managed to link twentieth-century England not only with ancient Egypt but with prehistoric Wessex.

ST PETER'S CHURCH MARLBOROUGH

In *c.* 1702 Celia Fiennes visited Marlborough and remarked that it 'looks very fine, with a good river that turns many mills; its buildings are good and compact, one very large street where stands the Market Place and Town Hall and at each end the two churches'. The Perpendicular-style church of St Peter and St Paul, declared redundant in 1974, stands at the southern end of the broad main street, while the parish church of St Mary, dating from Norman times, stands at the northern end. Fire devastated the town in 1653, destroying much of St Mary's but leaving St Peter's unscathed. After two further fires in 1679 and 1690, thatch was banned in the town by an Act of Parliament. The river that Fiennes refers to is the Kennet. She also noted that the Duke of Somerset's house was being built. Today, known as C-House, it forms part of Marlborough College, founded in 1843 as a public school. On the college grounds is a Neolithic mound like Silbury Hill, but only half as high. Legend says that it was the burial place of Merlin. Although it is now tree-covered, a sketch by Stukeley of 1723 shows it supporting a hanging garden and grotto.

BARBURY CASTLE

Five miles south of Swindon on the northern edge of Marlborough Downs are the earthwork remains of Barbury Castle, an Iron Age hill-fort defended by a double bank and ditches with entrances at the east and west. The earthworks to the south of the fort are thought to be all that remains of the lost medieval village of Berebury. On Burderop Down, to the east of the fort, are Celtic field systems covering about 140 acres. They were probably cultivated during the Iron Age, remaining in use into Roman times. An enclosure, possibly medieval, overlays the fields. Barbury Castle is linked to another hill-fort, Liddington Castle (formerly Badbury Castle), by the Ridgeway long-distance footpath. Both sites were favourite haunts of two Wiltshire writers, Richard Jefferies (1848-87) and Alfred Williams (1877-1931), who are commemorated on Burderop Down by a sarsen stone that was erected in 1939. Jefferies' birthplace at Coate, near Swindon, is now a museum. The photograph was taken from Barbury Castle looking south-east towards the beech clumps on Hackpen Hill.

DEVIL'S DEN
CLATFORD BOTTOM

Three miles east of Avebury in Clatford Bottom, near Fyfield, the Devil's Den is all that remains of a Neolithic long barrow. Re-erected in 1921, the two upright sarsen stones surmounted by a large capstone are thought to be a false entrance or a burial chamber. Two wall stones lie beneath the structure. The site is reputedly the den of a ghostly white dog with huge burning eyes. It is also said that on some nights the devil can be seen trying to move the stones with the help of four white oxen. Three miles southwest of the Devil's Den, the Sanctuary on Overton Hill is estimated to be 5000 years old. Originally linked to Avebury by the West Kennett Avenue, it appears to have been a round wooden structure, possibly a shrine. This was later surrounded by a larger and more complex building, which was subsequently enclosed by a double circle of stones. William Stukeley made a record of the 'temple' before it was destroyed and mostly ploughed over in 1724 'to gain a dirty little profit'. It was relocated by Maud Cunnington in 1930 and concrete posts now mark the position of the circular buildings.

BARBER STONE
AVEBURY

On 7 January 1649 John Aubrey, the antiquarian, was following the hunt through the village of Avebury when, as he put it, 'I was wonderfully surprised at the sight of those vast stones: of which I had never heard before: as also at the mighty bank and graff [ditch] about it: I observed in the enclosures some segments of rude circles, made with these stones; whence I concluded, they had been in the old time complete.' The first to recognize Avebury's prehistoric importance, Aubrey wrote that 'it did as much excel Stonehenge, as a cathedral does a parish church'. Charles II, hearing of the 'stupendous antiquity', visited the site in 1663 and 'commanded' Aubrey to 'write a description of it'. In the intervening centuries many of the stones were broken up and used as local building material. During excavation and restoration in 1938 Alexander Keiller discovered the skeleton of a fourteenth-century barber-surgeon, who had been accidentally crushed by a stone.

PASSAGE AND END-CHAMBER WEST KENNETT LONG BARROW

Two miles south of Avebury, the West Kennett Long Barrow, 340 feet long and 75 feet wide, is one of the largest and best-preserved Neolithic burial chambers in Britain. In 1685 Dr Robert Toope, a physician, wrote to his friend John Aubrey about his discoveries at the nearby Sanctuary, where he had found workmen digging up bones: 'I quickly perceived that they were human and came the next day and dug for them, and stored myself with many bushels, of which I made a noble medicine that relieved many of my distressed neighbours.' It seemed that Toope extended his search for bones to the West Kennett Long Barrow, causing much damage by his diggings. The stone-built central passage and end-chamber were excavated in 1859 by John Thurnam, who missed the four small burial chambers (two on either side) that were revealed in 1955-6 by Stuart Piggott and Richard Atkinson. From these discoveries it is known that over a period of at least 1500 years 46 individuals were buried in the barrow. Radiocarbon dating has indicated that the tomb was in use from *c.* 3700 BC.

SILBURY HILL

Standing 130 feet high and covering an area of over five acres, Silbury Hill is the largest artificial mound in Europe. But despite more than two centuries of investigation, its purpose remains a mystery. Dating from *c.* 2700 BC, the mound does not appear to have been used for burial. It was built in three stages over a relatively short period. The first mound, lying on a natural terrace, was formed from layers of gravel, turf, soil, clay and chalk; it was eighteen feet high with a base diameter of 120 feet. Soon after, a larger mound was built over it with chalk rubble dug from around the base to partially create a deep surrounding ditch: 40 feet wide, twenty feet deep and 350 feet in diameter. Before stage two was completed, a third mound was constructed over it; the first ditch was filled in and a larger one created, the excavated material being used in the building of the final mound, 520 feet in diameter. The construction was careful and precise, using chalk blocks to create six huge horizontal steps, which (except for the top) were later filled in with a mixture of chalk rubble and silt to produce the present outline.

WHITE HORSE CHERHILL

In 1780, on a steep slope beneath the earthen ramparts of Oldbury Castle, Dr Christopher Alsop, sometimes referred to as the 'mad doctor' of Calne, cut the Cherhill White Horse. 123 feet long and 131 feet high, it is reputed to have had an eye four feet in diameter filled with glass bottles to catch the sunlight. Camouflaged during World War II, the horse was uncovered in 1945 and resurfaced with a mixture of chalk and cement. A booklet entitled *Cherhill Village Remembered*, produced by Nancy Grafton and Margery Jenkins in 1990, contains descriptions and anecdotes about village life between the two world wars – a time when the roads were unsurfaced, when almost every villager kept a few pigs in a sty, when rubbish was buried in a corner of the garden, when the only water came from the local spring, and when 75 pounds could purchase three terraced houses. One farmer also recalls how he came to plough up a small field that was 'covered with bee orchids, which even in those days were becoming rare'.

VALE OF PEWSEY
from GIANT'S GRAVE

A local tradition holds that if a person runs seven times around the Giant's Grave, a promontory-fort above the village of Oare, the giant will appear. The photograph was taken from the grave looking east across the Vale of Pewsey towards the village of Wootton Rivers, where instead of numerals one of the clock faces of the church uses the letters GLORY BE TO GOD. The clock is also unusual in that it was built out of scrap metal – prams, bedsteads and other junk – by Jack Spratt to commemorate the coronation of George V in 1911. The Kennet and Avon canal, which passes through the village, is over 86 miles long and runs from the Thames at Reading to Hanham lock on the Bristol Avon. Navigation downstream of Hanham is tidal and leads, via the River Avon and Bristol's Floating Harbour, to Avonmouth and the Severn estuary. Martinsell Hill, which like the Giant's Grave overlooks Wootton Rivers, supports the earthwork remains of a rectangular Iron Age hill-fort. The purpose of the pit trenches on the hill are a mystery, but it has been suggested that they were used to store grain during the Bronze Age.

EAST STREET
LACOCK

The village of Lacock, on the
west bank of the Bristol Avon,
was given to the National Trust
in 1944, and much of it, therefore, lacks such twentieth-century
eyesores as television aerials,
telephone wires and yellow lines.
Built from the profits of the
medieval wool trade, Lacock contains an attractive cluster of
stone, red-brick and half-tim-
bered cottages dating from the
thirteenth to the nineteenth century. On the corner of East Street
is a fourteenth-century tithe barn.
Adjoining it is an eighteenth-
century domed Lock-up, or Blind
House. The Fox Talbot Museum,
near the entrance to Lacock
Abbey, commemorates the
achievements of the pioneer pho-
tographer. Among the oldest
houses in the village are King
John's Hunting Lodge, said to be
older than the abbey, and the
fourteenth-century Cruck House.

TOWN BRIDGE
BRADFORD-ON-AVON

In *c.* 1540 John Leland wrote that
'all the town of Bradford standith
by cloth making'. Daniel Defoe
noted in 1724 that the clothiers in
and around Bradford-on-Avon –
a major centre of woollen cloth
manufacture – were worth 'from
ten thousand, to forty thousand
pounds a man'. The city's afflu-
ence is reflected in its wealth of
fine stone houses that rise up the
steep hillside on the north bank
of the Avon, especially those
built in the early eighteenth century. Even at the beginning of the
nineteenth century it had 32 cloth
factories, excluding the looms in
the weavers' cottages. The thirteenth-century Town Bridge,
widened in the seventeenth century, supports a small domed
'chapel' (at left), used as a lock-
up and possibly a toll-house. The
fish weather-vane on top gave
rise to the saying that those in
prison were 'under the fish and
over the water'. Among the many
buildings of interest are the
parish church of Holy Trinity;
The Hall, a mansion built by
John Hall, a clothier, around
1610; Westbury House, scene of
a riot against the introduction of
new machinery in 1791; and the
chapel of St Mary, Tory.

TITHE BARN
BRADFORD-ON-AVON

The great stone tithe barn at Barton Farm, on the southern outskirts of Bradford-on-Avon, was built in the early fourteenth century for Shaftesbury Abbey, the largest and richest Benedictine nunnery in England; so rich, in fact, that it gave rise to the saying: 'If the abbot of Glastonbury could marry the abbess of Shaftesbury their heir would hold more land than the king of England.' The slate-roofed barn is 168 feet long and over 30 feet wide, with four porches and a magnificent timber roof of fourteen bays. Now in the care of English Heritage, the barn is only one of the gems of Bradford-on-Avon. The greatest is the church of St Laurence, forgotten for centuries and redis-covered in 1856. Converted into a cottage and school with buildings attached, it was found to be one of the best-preserved Anglo-Saxon churches in England, dating from the tenth century and possibly earlier. Restored and cleared of all the extraneous building, the church – with its two bas-relief angels – is reputed to stand on the side of a little church (*ecclesiola*) founded by St Aldehelm in *c.* 700.

GREAT CHALFIELD MANOR
near HOLT

Built of local honey-coloured stone by Thomas Tropnell, a wealthy landowner, in 1465-80 to replace an earlier fortified building, Great Chalfield Manor is considered to be one of the finest late-medieval manor houses in England. After suffering two centuries of neglect and disrepair, the ruins were sensitively restored in 1905-12. For his reconstruction Sir Harold Brakspear, the architect, referred to drawings made in 1836 by Thomas Larkin Walker, a pupil of Pugin. Although the property has a moat and fishpond, it was never completely encircled by water. A mural in the dining room, revealed in 1908, is thought to be a contemporary portrait of Tropnell. Interestingly, he has five fingers and one thumb on each hand. Pevsner draws attention to the three 'curious' little spy windows in the great hall which are 'given the form of masks with open mouths and eyes – a bishop, the devil and another face . . . a feature almost unique in England'. The fourteenth-century parish church of All Saints was given a bell-cote and spire by Tropnell. The manor, like The Courts at Holt, is owned by the National Trust.

WHITE HORSE
WESTBURY

The earliest white horse hill-figure in England is situated on the chalk escarpment beneath the Iron Age hill-fort of Uffington Castle in Oxfordshire. Thought to date from *c.* 50 BC, it faces right, unlike most other white horses. Periodic 'scouring' of the horse has maintained the figure more or less in its original form over some 2000 years. Its purpose is unknown, but experts suggest that it may have been the emblem of the Atrebates, a tribe from Belgic Gaul (northern France) who occupied the hill-fort in the first century BC. The white horse on the steep western slope of Westbury Hill, below the Iron Age hill-fort of Bratton Castle, was cut into the turf in 1778. It replaced an earlier horse said to have been cut to com-memorate King Alfred's victory over the Danes at Ethandun (pos-sibly nearby Edington) in 878. 'Rectified' in 1873, it now looks, in Nikolaus Pevsner's words, 'a moderately correct, dispirited ani-mal'. Some 166 feet long and 163 feet high, the horse, which faces left, no longer needs regular scouring, as it has been pre-served by concrete.

PARISH CHURCH
BRATTON

High above the village of Bratton, the parish church of St James stands in peaceful isolation amid the trees and turf of the downland escarpment. Apart from the chancel and vestry (rebuilt in 1854 and 1925 respec-tively), the church is mainly in the Perpendicular style, dating from *c.* 1400. The village was originally three hamlets: Little Stoke by the church, Milbourne by the mill-stream and Bratton, 'a clearing in the forest'. Local tradi-tion says that the houses of Little Stoke fell into ruin and disap-peared after most of the inhabi-tants had been wiped out by plague. Records state that there was a manor house near the church, but, like the houses, it ceased to exist by 1640. Housing development in the 1970s finally merged Bratton with Milbourne. Bratton Castle, an Iron Age hill-fort protected on three sides by steep slopes, occupies 25 acres of the flat plateau south-west of the village. Within its massive defen-sive banks and ditches is a dam-aged Neolithic long barrow – 230 feet long, 65 feet wide and twelve feet high – in which two partly burnt human skeletons were found.

PRIORY CHURCH EDINGTON

In 1351 William of Edington, Bishop of Winchester, founded a college of chantry priests at the place of his birth, Edington. Seven years later it became a Bonshommes monastery, one of only two such Augustinian monasteries in England (the first having been founded some seventy years earlier at Ashridge, Hertfordshire). The priory church, built on the site of a Norman foundation, was begun in 1352 and consecrated in 1361. Cruciform in plan, the battlemented church is important architecturally, as it marks the transition from the Decorated to the Perpendicular style. During Jack Cade's rebellion in 1450, the Bishop of Salisbury, William Ayscough, was dragged from the church by a mob and brutally murdered. After the Dissolution, the priory – dedicated to St Mary, St Katherine and All Saints – became a parish church. Nothing else survives of the monastic buildings. Edington is thought by some to be the site of the battle of Ethandun, fought in 878, in which King Alfred defeated the Danes. Others, however, claim that the place referred to by the old chronicles is Edington, near Westonzoyland, on the Polden Hills.

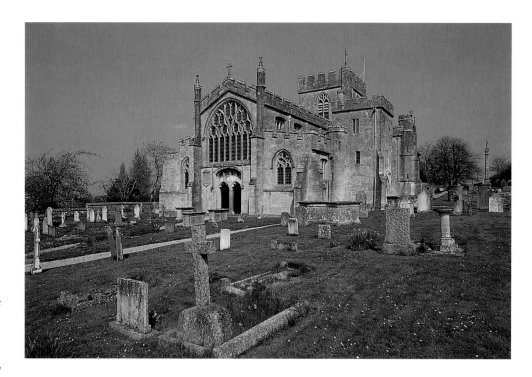

THE PANTHEON STOURHEAD GARDEN

Not far from the source of the River Stour, the wealthy banker Henry Hoare II began around 1744 to lay out one of the finest 'Arcadian' landscape gardens in England. Over forty years he created a vast lake out of a series of medieval fishponds, planted rare species of trees and plants, and erected classical temples, bridges, grottoes and monuments. Glimpsed from various aspects through the trees, the central focus of the gardens is the Pantheon (right), erected in 1753-4 and designed by Henry Flitcroft, architect of most of the grounds' buildings. A medieval cross was removed from the city of Bristol and erected at Stourhead in 1765. The Palladian Bridge (foreground) was built in 1762. Its road surface is covered in turf. Stourhead House was designed in 1721 for Henry Hoare I by Colen Campbell in the Palladian style. Among the works of art, it contains furniture by Thomas Chippendale the Younger. The estate is now owned by the National Trust. Visitors to the house should try to avoid peak viewing times, especially weekends, as it can become extremely crowded.

WHITE SHEET HILL
near MERE

At the western edge of Salisbury Plain, two miles north-west of the medieval market town of Mere, is the chalk grassland of Whitesheet Hill, part of the Stourhead Estate, which was given to the National Trust in 1946. Since 1964 a small area has been managed as a nature reserve by the Wiltshire Trust for Nature Conservation. On the 802-foot summit are the earthwork remains of an Iron Age hill-fort. On the western spur of the hill, overlooking the Stourhead Estate, is a Neolithic causewayed camp covering some four acres. The oval enclosure is defined by a rampart and outer ditch interrupted by over twenty undug gaps or causeways. It is partly over-lapped by a large Bronze Age round barrow. A number of Iron Age cross-dykes can also be found on the ridge. The photo-graph was taken from White Sheet Hill looking north across farmland to Long Knoll and Little Knoll. About a mile south-east, on the steep sides of the down-land above Mere, are the remains of an agricultural system known as strip lynchets, thought to have originated in Romano-British times. The terraces were still in use during the Middle Ages.

KING ALFRED'S TOWER STOURTON

Across the border on Kingsettle Hill in Somerset, at the edge of the Stourhead Estate, stands the 160-foot-high red-brick folly known as King Alfred's Tower, built by Henry Flitcroft for Henry Hoare II and completed in 1772. A prominent landmark, the trian-gular tower has a viewing plat-form at the top, reached by a spi-ral staircase inside one of the cor-ner turrets. Above the door is a statue of King Alfred and a plaque that reads: 'Alfred the Great AD 879 on this summit erected his standard against Danish invaders. To him we owe the origin of juries, the establish-ment of a militia, the creation of a naval force. Alfred the light of a benighted age was a philosopher and a Christian, the father of his people, the founder of the English monarchy and liberty.' A Mosquito aircraft on a low-flying exercise during World War II struck the tower. The damage it caused is shown by the lighter-coloured bricks used in the repair. The tower is open to the public at certain times.

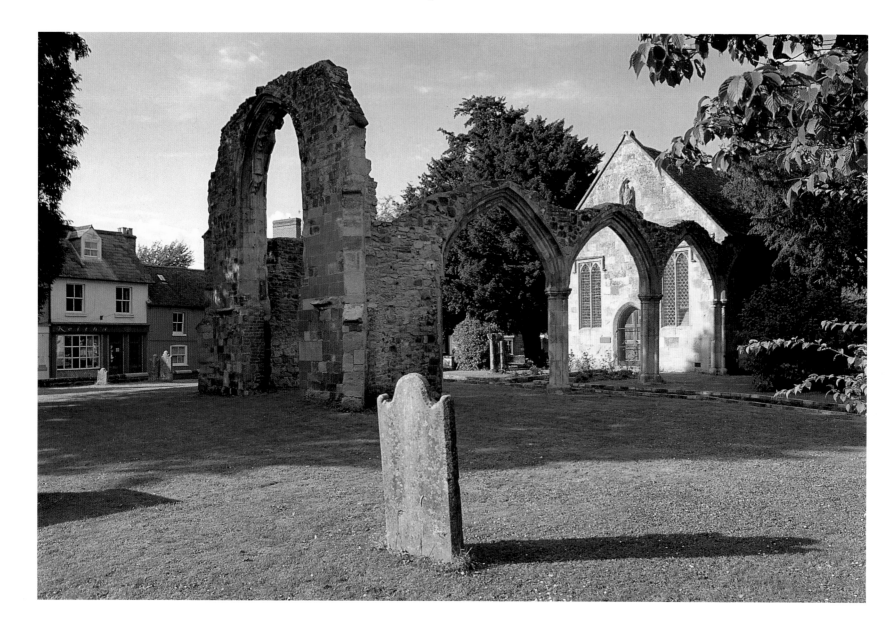

ST MARY'S CHURCH WILTON

Situated at the confluence of the rivers Wylye and Nadder, the market town of Wilton was once the capital of Saxon Wessex and the original county town of Wiltshire. The nunnery, established in 830 by Egbert, King of Wessex, was refounded by Alfred the Great in 890. After the Dissolution, Henry VIII granted the abbey buildings to William Herbert, 1st Earl of Pembroke, who built Wilton House on the site. Rebuilt by Philip Herbert, the 4th Earl, in the 1630s, the house was gutted by fire in 1647 and again reconstructed with magnificent state rooms designed by Inigo Jones. In 1801 the 11th Earl commissioned James Wyatt to remodel the house, which involved much rebuilding. Home of the Earl of Pembroke, the house and gardens are open to the public. The parish church of St Mary and St Nicholas was built in 1841-5 by the 1st Lord Herbert of Lea, son of the 11th Earl. It was one of the first churches in England to be built in the Lombardic style and replaced the medieval parish church of St Mary, which except for the chantry is now a ruin. The town is also noted for its carpets.

SALISBURY CATHEDRAL

The origins of the cathedral city of Salisbury lie two miles to the north on the hill-top settlement site of Old Sarum, where there have been a prehistoric fort, a Roman stronghold and an Anglo-Saxon borough with a mint. After the Norman Conquest, a motte-and-bailey castle was built at the centre of the mound. A thriving town developed around the castle, which became a bishopric in 1075, when the see was transferred from Sherborne. The first cathedral was largely destroyed by a storm within five days of its consecration in 1092. Bishop Roger, consecrated in 1107, not only rebuilt the cathedral but received permission to reconstruct the royal castle, part of which he turned into his own palace. Conflict between the clerics and the military, together with a site that was found to be too windy and waterless, led to the see being moved from Old Sarum to New Sarum (Salisbury) in the valley below. The city – laid out on a medieval grid pattern – grew up and prospered around the new cathedral, built mostly between 1220 and 1258. The spire, the tallest in England at 404 feet, was added in the fourteenth century.

STONEHENGE

In *The History of the Kings of Britain* (*c.* 1136) Geoffrey of Monmouth ascribes the creation of Stonehenge to Merlin, who uses his magical powers to bring the giant stones from Ireland to Salisbury Plain. Fact, however, maintains that the monument dates from Neolithic times and was built in three principal phases. The first was the construction in about 3000 BC of a large circular earthwork used as a place of worship and burial. The second stage occurred some 1000 years later, when bluestones from the Preseli Mountains in south-west Wales were used to create a 'temple' with an entrance in the north-east, approached along a processional 'avenue' aligned with the direction of the midsummer sunrise. The final stage, started soon after, was the creation of a fully lintelled stone circle with sarsen boulders from the Marlborough Downs. Inside the 100-foot-diameter circle, the bluestones were re-arranged to form a smaller circle, within which two horseshoe forms were erected, one of bluestones and the other of sarsens. Although badly ruined today, Stonehenge continues to conceal the mystery of its real purpose.

WOODHENGE
near AMESBURY

Two miles north-east of Stonehenge is the site known as 'Dough Cover', long considered to be a large disc barrow that was mutilated by ploughing. While flying over the area in 1925, however, Squadron Leader Insall noticed a series of round marks within a large circle. Excavations carried out by B. H. and M. E. Cunnington between 1926 and 1928 revealed that the site was in fact a Neolithic henge monument dating from *c.* 2300 BC. It consisted of six concentric oval rings formed by timber posts (their positions now marked by concrete pillars), enclosed by an irregular circular ditch and bank. The long axis of the ovals are aligned towards the midsummer sunrise. Entry to the monument, which may have been roofed, was by a causeway to the north-east. Near the centre of the structure, the excavations also revealed the grave of a small child who had died from a blow to the skull; the spot is now marked by a cairn of flints. Because of its similarity to Stonehenge, the monument was jokingly referred to as Woodhenge, a name that happened to stick.

VALE OF PEWSEY
from KNAP HILL

On Knap Hill, overlooking the Vale of Pewsey, is a Neolithic causewayed camp covering about four acres. On the east side of the camp are the earthwork remains of an Iron Age enclosure. To the west of the camp, on the slopes of the 952-foot Milk Hill, is a white horse cut by Robert Pile of Alton Barnes around 1812. It is said that he paid twenty pounds to John Thorne, a journeyman-painter, to carry out the task. Thorne hired someone else to do the actual work, then disappeared with the money before the horse was finished. He was eventually hanged, presumably for a more serious crime. On Walker's Hill, between the horse and the camp, Adam's Grave long barrow dates from around 2000 BC. Excavations in 1860 revealed a number of human skeletons. The ancient Ridgeway track crosses the great Wansdyke less than a mile north of Knap Hill. In AD 592 the *Anglo Saxon Chronicle* records that 'there was great slaughter in Britain this year at Adam's Grave, and Ceawlin [King of Wessex] was expelled'. A two-edged sword found at Knap Hill and now in Devizes Museum may be a relic of this battle.

LUDGERSHALL CASTLE

On his way to the 'rotten borough' of Ludgershall on the evening of Sunday, 27 August 1826, William Cobbett and his horse were plagued by troublesome flies. 'I was obliged to carry a great bough, and to keep it in constant motion, in order to make the horse peaceable enough to enable me to keep on his back.' The small market town, which Cobbett called 'one of the most mean and beggarly places that man ever set eyes on', contains the ruins of a castle dating back to the reign of Henry I (1100-35). The earthwork remains of timber-strengthened ramparts, however, are thought to date from the late eleventh century. During the thirteenth century, the castle was a popular royal hunting palace, rather than a fortress, but by the mid-sixteenth century it was in ruins. The castle remains and the stump of a late-medieval cross, in the main street of the village, are in the care of English Heritage. The Norman church of St James contains a monument to Sir Richard Brydges (d. 1558) and his wife, Jane, which Pevsner describes as 'one of the most important of its date in England'.

Winchester and Hampshire

Beacon Hill, one of a number of hills bearing this name, is located six miles south of Newbury. On its summit are the earthwork remains of an Iron Age contour fort, within which are about fifteen hut-hollows, each some 30 feet in diameter. Also on the summit is the grave of the 5th Earl of Carnarvon, former owner of the hill. While excavating in Egypt with Howard Carter, he discovered Tutankhamen's tomb but died in 1923 from blood poisoning after a mosquito bite. He was born in 1866 at nearby Highclere Castle, designed in the 1830s by Charles Barry, architect of the Houses of Parliament. Home of the Earl and Countess of Carnarvon, the Victorian mansion and its parkland laid out by Capability Brown in the 1770s are open to the public. Three miles to the east of Beacon Hill is Watership Down, the setting of Richard Adams' story of rabbits. Midway between Watership Down and Beacon Hill stands Ladle Hill, the site of an unfinished Iron Age hill-fort. Also on the hill is a large Bronze Age disc-barrow, 170 feet in diameter.

Roman city of *Venta Belgarum*, royal residence and cathedral city of *Wintanceastre*, administrative centre of Wessex, and from the tenth century, the capital of Anglo-Saxon and Danish England – an honour that it shared with London for some 200 years after the Norman Conquest – Winchester has an undeniably rich history. It also maintained close links with the Crown until the reign of Charles II (1660-85), when the king abandoned plans to build a royal palace to rival Versailles on the site of the medieval castle. The unfinished mansion, designed by Sir Christopher Wren, burnt down in 1894. This ancient city was founded at an important crossing of the River Itchen in a fold of the Hampshire downs, a location that prompted William Cobbett to write in 1825: 'There are not many finer spots in England . . . Here are hill, dell, water, meadows, woods, cornfields, downs; and all of them very fine and very beautifully disposed.'

Winchester's dramatic rise to prominence, however, was essentially due to one person – the most celebrated of all Anglo-Saxon kings, the military leader who successfully stemmed the tide of Danish conquest, the initiator of a far-reaching programme of military reform and cultural revival, the law-maker, scholar and translator of certain Latin books into English (in his own words, 'the language we can all understand') and the man who will forever be popularly remembered as having 'burnt the cakes' – Alfred the Great, King of Wessex, whose eventful reign marked the beginning of England as a single nation under one king.

Born at Wantage, Oxfordshire, in 849 during a time when the country was threatened by Viking and Danish incursions, Alfred was the youngest son of Ethelwulf, King of Wessex, and brother of Ethelred, whom he succeeded to the throne in 871. Seven years of bitter fighting against the Danes led to Alfred's defeat at the battle of Chippenham and his retreat into the watery wastes of the Somerset Levels. From his fortified base on the Isle of Athelney, Alfred waged guerrilla war upon the Danes, while gradually gathering about him a strong army of supporters. It was while Alfred was living like an outlaw at Athelney that he sought shelter in a cottage and was scolded by the woman for allowing the cakes she was baking to burn. By May 878 the fugitive king was ready to openly challenge the might of the Danish army under their leader, Guthrum.

In what was to be the decisive battle of the war, the opposing forces met at Ethandun

(Edington). Guthrum was totally defeated and made to sign a peace treaty at Wedmore, south of Axbridge. Under the terms of this agreement Guthrum agreed to be baptised a Christian, taking the Anglo-Saxon name Athelstan, and to leave Wessex and remain in the territory east of Watling Street, later to be known as the Danelaw. Guthrum and his men settled in East Anglia, where he kept peace with Alfred and reigned as king until his death in 890. Taking advantage of the respite from fighting, Alfred set about strengthening the borders of Wessex. He created a series of fortified strongholds, or *burhs*, stretching from East Sussex to Devon; reorganized his army, or *fyrd*, by dividing his 'levies into two sections, so that there was always half at home and half on active service, with the exception of those men whose duty it was to man the fortresses' (*Anglo Saxon Chronicle*); and he built up a navy to challenge the Viking invaders on their own element, the sea, thereby forcing them to turn their attentions from England to northern France (later to become Normandy).

Winchester became Alfred's favoured residence, the administrative and cultural centre of a revitalized Anglo-Saxon Wessex, where law, order and learning were encouraged and the values of the Christian Church revived. The city's defences were strengthened, the old Roman walls rebuilt and the streets laid out in the present grid pattern.

After his death in 899 Alfred was buried in the Old Minster. Shortly after, his widow, Ealhswith, founded a Benedictine nunnery (Nunnaminster) in the city, and around 903 their son, Edward the Elder, established a monastery for monks (New Minster). Several mortuary chests within the present cathedral contain the bones of some of the early Kings of Wessex, among them Cynegils (reigned 611-43), the first Christian King of Wessex, and Ethelwulf (reigned 839-58), father of Alfred. Alfred's remains, however, are not among them. Despite a claim that they lie buried at Little Driffield church (north of Kingston upon Hull), it is generally accepted that they rest under a flat stone in the churchyard of St Bartholomew's church at Winchester.

Writing in the early twelfth century, the Anglo-Norman historian Orderic Vitalis pronounced a verdict on Alfred: 'the first king to hold sway over the whole of England. In goodness, nobility and statesmanship he stood, I believe, head and shoulders above all the kings of England who came before and after him.' In 1901 a massive bronze statue of the king by Hamo Thornycroft was erected on a prominent site in the heart of the ancient capital. Carved on the stone base' is a single, but poignant, word: Aelfred.

BISHOP'S PALACE BISHOP'S WALTHAM

Medieval seat of the wealthy Bishops of Winchester, the ruins of Bishop's Waltham Palace are located some nine miles south-east of Winchester. They date from two main rebuilding periods: the late twelfth century under bishops Henry of Blois (1129-1171) – younger brother of King Stephen – and probably Richard of Ilchester (1174-88); and the late fourteenth and early fifteenth centuries under bishops William of Wykeham (1367-1404) and his successor, Henry Beaufort (1404-47). John Leland wrote in the 1540s that 'the Bishop of Winchester hath a right ample and goodly manor about and a pretty brook running hard by it'. After the Dissolution, the bishops lost ownership of the palace until 1558, when it was restored to them by Queen Mary. A Royalist stronghold during the Civil War, it was destroyed by Parliamentarian forces after their victorious battle at Cheriton in 1644. From then on, though belonging to the bishops until 1869, the palace ceased to be their residence. The photograph looks north across the remains of the Bishop's great chamber and west tower to the hall and kitchen.

THE POINT
PORTSMOUTH HARBOUR

Outside both the early town walls and the law, the Point, with its narrow streets, taverns and inns, was a notoriously rough area. Today it is a fashionable place to live. Tower House was the home of the marine artist W. L. Wyllie from 1906-31, while Quebec House, built on the water's edge in 1754, was one of England's first sea-bathing houses. The medieval town and port of Portsmouth was founded by Richard I in the late twelfth century. As Southampton became the main commercial port of the Solent, Portsmouth developed into a heavily fortified naval and garrison town. In the early fifteenth century two wood towers were erected on opposite sides of the narrow harbour entrance to control a chain boom. The towers were later reconstructed in stone, but only the Round Tower on the Point survives. The oldest of the royal dockyards, Portsmouth boasts England's first permanent dry dock, built in 1496. Historic ships on display are HMS *Victory*, Nelson's flagship during the battle of Trafalgar; HMS *Warrior*, Britain's first ironclad warship; and the *Mary Rose*, a Tudor warship raised from the sea-bed in 1982.

SPITBANK FORT
from SOUTHSEA

One of three circular sea-forts guarding Spithead, the eastern entrance to the Solent, Spitbank Fort is the closest to Portsmouth. Like Horse Sand Fort and No Man's Land Fort, it was constructed in the 1860s and 1870s to protect the naval base and anchorage against enemy landings from the west. The defences were part of a ring of highly advanced self-contained forts completely surrounding Gosport and Portsmouth Harbour. Known as 'Palmerston Folly' after the then Prime Minister, the forts on the mainland included Fort Brockhurst, now owned by English Heritage, Fort Fareham, Fort Southwick and Fort Nelson. Like Spithead Fort, which has to be reached by boat, Fort Brockhurst and Fort Nelson are open to the public. The castle on the sea front at Southsea was built by Henry VIII in 1544 and later enlarged. The lighthouse was erected in the early 1820s. The castle is now a museum with displays on the military history of Portsmouth. It was from here, in July 1545, that the king watched in horror as his flagship the *Mary Rose*, fully manned and equipped for battle, capsized and sank, drowning some 400 to 700 men.

PORTSMOUTH CATHEDRAL

Founded in *c.* 1180 by Jean de Gisors, a wealthy merchant, the first church of St Thomas Becket was built by the canons of Southwick Priory. Originally a chapel to St Mary's at Kingston (the parish church of Portsea Island), it became the parish church of Old Portsmouth, within the diocese of Winchester, in 1320. In 1683-93, after suffering damage during the Civil War, the tower and nave were demolished and rebuilt. The octagonal wooden cupola was added in 1703, and during the nineteenth century the church was restored. In 1927 the diocese of Portsmouth was established and the parish church of St Thomas became a cathedral. Sir Charles Nicholson designed an extension to the church that doubled its size, while retaining the tower. The Red Lion, a tavern that also served as a brothel, was razed to make way for the new nave. Work was interrupted by the outbreak of World War II, and the partially completed nave simply bricked up. The cathedral remained unfinished until 1990, when building was resumed to plans by Michael Drury. It was completed the following year.

PORTCHESTER CASTLE

On a low promontory in Portsmouth Harbour stands the third-century Roman fort at Portchester, one of a series of forts built to protect the Channel coast from attack by Saxon invaders. Within a corner of its 20-foot-high walls – made from flint and mortar, strengthened with horizontal bonding courses of tile and limestone – the Normans constructed a castle, dominated by a tall square keep erected in the 1120s and later heightened. The castle was converted into a small palace by Richard II in 1396-9, the remains of which include the hall, kitchen and great chamber. It served as an embarkation point for soldiers who fought in the battle of Crecy (1346) under Edward III and in the battle of Agincourt (1415) under Henry V, and during the Napoleonic Wars it was used as a military prison – graffiti carved by the prisoners can be seen on the keep walls. Also on the site was a small Augustinian priory, founded in *c.* 1128. By 1150 the canons had moved to Southwick, nearby. The priory church, dedicated to St Mary and restored in 1706, still stands within the Roman walls.

TITCHFIELD ABBEY

Founded for Premonstratensian canons in 1232 by Bishop Peter des Roches, Titchfield Abbey, now in ruins, stands on the west side of the River Meon near Fareham. The abbey church witnessed the marriage of Henry VI and Margaret of Anjou in 1445. After its dissolution in 1537 the abbey was granted to Thomas Wriothesley (later 1st Earl of Southampton), who incorporated parts of the monastery into a private mansion, known as Place House. Leland wrote in *c.* 1540: 'Mr Wriothesley hath builded a right stately house embattled and having a goodly gate and a conduit casteled in the middle of the court of it, in the very same place where the late monastery of Premonstratensians stood.' Most of the house was demolished in 1781, but the shell of the 'goodly gate', fashioned out of the abbey church's nave, remains. Near the abbey is a timber-framed tithe barn, probably fifteenth century. The village of Titchfield was a medieval market centre and small port. In the parish church of St Peter, dating from Anglo-Saxon times, is a magnificent monument to Thomas Wriothesley, his wife and their son.

NETLEY ABBEY

Three miles south-east of Southampton city centre, on the north bank of Southampton Water, is Netley Abbey, founded in 1239 for Cistercian monks from Beaulieu by Peter des Roches, Bishop of Winchester (1205-38), and Henry III, who assumed the duties of founder-patron in 1251. After its dissolution in 1536 the abbey and grounds were granted to Sir William Paulet (later 1st Marquis of Winchester), who converted the church into a private mansion. The house was sold in the eighteenth century to a Southampton builder, but demolition was halted when he was killed by falling masonry. Netley Castle, near the abbey, is a Victorian house incorporating a small fort built by Henry VIII in 1542. In the nearby Royal Victoria Country Park are the remains of the quarter-mile-long Royal Victoria Military Hospital, founded in 1856. The chapel is now a museum. The village of Netley grew up between the abbey and the hospital and dates from the mid-nineteenth century. The church of St Edward the Confessor, built in 1886, contains part of the tomb of a medieval knight, which was originally in the abbey.

TOWN QUAY
SOUTHAMPTON

At the head of Southampton
Water on a broad peninsula
between the estuaries of the
rivers Test and Itchen, medieval
Southampton was protected by a
stone wall with 29 towers and
eight gates, much of which survives. As the town's suburbs
expanded in Victorian times, the
site of *Clausentum*, the Roman
naval base (near Bitterne), was
built over. The original Saxon
town of *Hamwic*, or *Hamtun*,
occupied an area around St
Mary's church outside the walled
town. After the Norman
Conquest, Southampton developed into a major port, trading
with countries in Europe and
around the Mediterranean. The
Norman castle had its own quay,
where French wine was
unloaded and stored in its vault.
Built in the 1180s by Henry II,
the vault is the only part of the
castle still intact. Until the French
raid of 1338, the wealthy merchants – English, French and
Italian – used the West Quay to
load and unload their goods.
From the 1400s Town Quay
became the town's main port
until the building of the docks in
the 1840s. Today Southampton is
a major container port with a
ferry service to the Isle of Wight.

MERCHANT'S HOUSE
SOUTHAMPTON

After miraculously surviving the
heavy bombing that flattened
much of ancient Southampton
during World War II, the timber-
framed Medieval Merchant's
House in French Street has been
carefully restored and furnished
to resemble its mid-fourteenth
century appearance. Built in
c. 1290, it was one of over 60
similar dwellings crowded within
the walls of the medieval town.
The merchant who originally
owned the house sold cider,
beer, wine and spices (the latter
two can still be purchased in the
reconstructed shop today).
French Street received its name
from the merchants who settled
in the south-west quarter of the
town after the Norman Conquest.
Other buildings of interest
include the three-storeyed God's
House Tower, built in the early
fifteenth century; the Tudor
House Museum occupied by
Richard Lyster, Lord Chief Justice
of the King's Bench from 1546 to
1552; St Michael's church dating
from 1070; the fourteenth-century
Wool House of Beaulieu Abbey,
now the Maritime Museum; the
Tudor Merchant's Hall beside
the West Gate; and the ruins of
the Holy Rood church, dating
from 1320.

ROMSEY ABBEY

In *c.* 907 Edward the Elder founded the monastery at Romsey, but it was refounded in 967 for Benedictine nuns by King Edgar. Badly damaged by the Danes around 993, the nuns were forced to flee to Winchester. The present building was begun during the reign of Henry I, probably in the 1120s, but additions and alterations continued over the centuries. In 1544, after the Dissolution, the town purchased the abbey church and saved it from destruction. One of its treasures is the illuminated Romsey psalter of 1440. In the south transept, known as St Nicholas Chapel, is the grave of Earl Mountbatten of Burma, assassinated on 27 August 1979 while on holiday in Ireland. A bomb, hidden in his fishing boat, *Shadow V*, also killed his fourteen-year-old grandson, the 83-year-old Dowager Lady Brabourne and the fifteen-year-old boat boy. Broadlands, the home of Lord Mountbatten, is open to the public. It was also the home of Lord Palmerston, who was Prime Minister in 1855-8 and 1859-65. King John's House, about 100 yards east of the abbey, contains medieval graffiti, including a caricature of Edward I.

MOTTISFONT ABBEY

Delightfully situated on the west bank of the River Test, the priory of Mottisfont, dedicated to the Holy Trinity, was founded in 1201 for Augustinian canons by William Briwere, or Brewer. Despite being a small establishment, it was chosen as the burial place of Maud of Lancaster, John of Gaunt's daughter, and boasted the forefinger of St John the Baptist. Any hopes of it becoming a prosperous foundation ended with the arrival of the Black Death, which devastated the community. Towards the end of the fifteenth century, the house could only maintain three canons. After the Dissolution, the monastic estate was granted to the Lord Chamberlain, William Lord Sandys, who started to build a mansion on the site, which was completed later by the 2nd and 3rd Lord Sandys. The present house, incorporating parts of the priory and Tudor mansion, was built in the mid-eighteenth century. The drawing room was decorated by Rex Whistler in 1938-9. The gardens are famous for the national collection of old-fashioned roses, but access to the house, owned by the National Trust, is limited.

PARISH CHURCH
QUARLEY

The parish church of St Michael, some five miles south of Ludgershall, dates from Anglo-Saxon times (possibly the ninth century) and is mentioned in the Domesday Book of 1086. After the Norman Conquest the church was rebuilt but retained parts of the Saxon building. Further reconstruction took place over the centuries – enlargement of the chancel in the fifteenth century and major restoration between 1878 and 1882, when a south porch was added. The east window (at right), with square Ionic pillars inside and out, was inserted in 1723 and is one of the earliest examples of a Venetian window in England. According to the inscription, the window was built by William Benson and Henry Hoare of Stourhead, both leading exponents of the English Palladian movement. Although Henry Hoare II was Lord of the Manor of Quarley at the time, the benefactor referred to may be his father, Henry Hoare I. The bells are unusual in that they hang not inside a bell-turret but outside in a frame at ground level on the north side of the church.

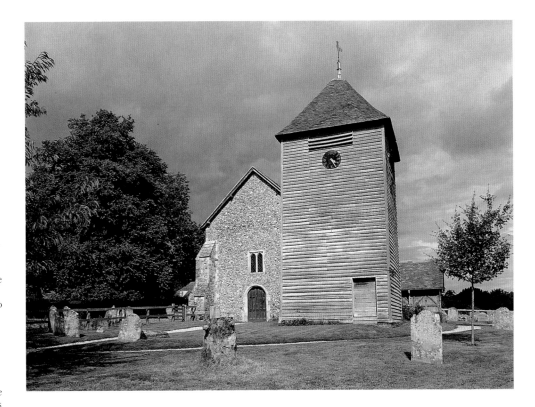

PARISH CHURCH
MICHELMERSH

The parish church of St Mary at Michelmersh, built in the late twelfth or early thirteenth century on the site of an Anglo-Saxon foundation and extensively restored in 1847, is noted for its unusual wood tower. The once detached timber tower, with its pyramid roof, was added in the fifteenth century, but the external weather-boarding has been renewed several times. The stone knight lying in the chancel with a stag at his feet is thought to be Sir Geoffrey de Canterton, 'Forester to the King in the New Forest *c.* 1320'. There is also a small tablet that depicts the separate kneeling figures of Trustram Fantleroy (d. 1538) and his wife, Johan, as well as a memorial to the Royalist Sir William Ogle, Viscount Caterlough, who died in 1682. He was Governor of Winchester Castle at the beginning of the Civil War. His ghost is said to ride through the village, either on a horse or in a carriage. In 1415 over 600 knights and archers reputedly camped in the field south of the church on their way to France and the battle of Agincourt.

HILL COTTAGE
MONXTON

In the valley of the Pilhill Brook, three miles west of Andover, the village of Monxton contains many attractive thatched cottages, such as Hill Cottage. The flint-and-stone church, dedicated to St Mary, was built in 1854 to replace a previous building considered by the surveyor to be 'absolutely dangerous'. The twelfth-century capitals of the Norman church that once stood on the site have been preserved in the present chancel arch. A brass plaque on the north wall is dedicated to Alice Swayne, who died in 1599 at the age of 98. Her son, Arthur, who died in 1609 and is buried in the churchyard, was a tenant of King's College, Cambridge (originally the College of the Blessed Mary and St Nicholas, which had been granted the manor of Monxton by Henry VI at its foundation in 1441). Arthur Mee mentions that an early eighteenth-century rector had 'such a mania for mathematics that he took no interest in anything else, never leaving his house to carry out his duties in church, nor giving himself time to be shaved'.

THE ESTATE OFFICE
ENHAM ALAMEIN

After World War I the hamlet of Enham, north of Andover, was used as a major rehabilitation centre for gassed and wounded ex-servicemen. At the outbreak of World War II, disabled men and women helped the war effort by manufacturing Nissen huts and barrage balloons, although they were already profitably employed in industries like basket-weaving and cabinet-making. Following the donation of a large sum of money to the Enham Village Centre by Egypt – as an expression of gratitude for their deliverance at the battle of El Alamein in 1942 – the village greatly expanded. Houses were specially built for the disabled, and the village was renamed Enham Alamein. The present church of St George, consecrated in 1974, is full of memorials to the units that took part in the North African battle. The three stained-glass windows in the Memorial Chapel are dedicated to the Mediterranean Fleet 1942, the 8th Army, and the Western Desert Air Force. The Estate Office, on a large green near the church, also contains a small museum.

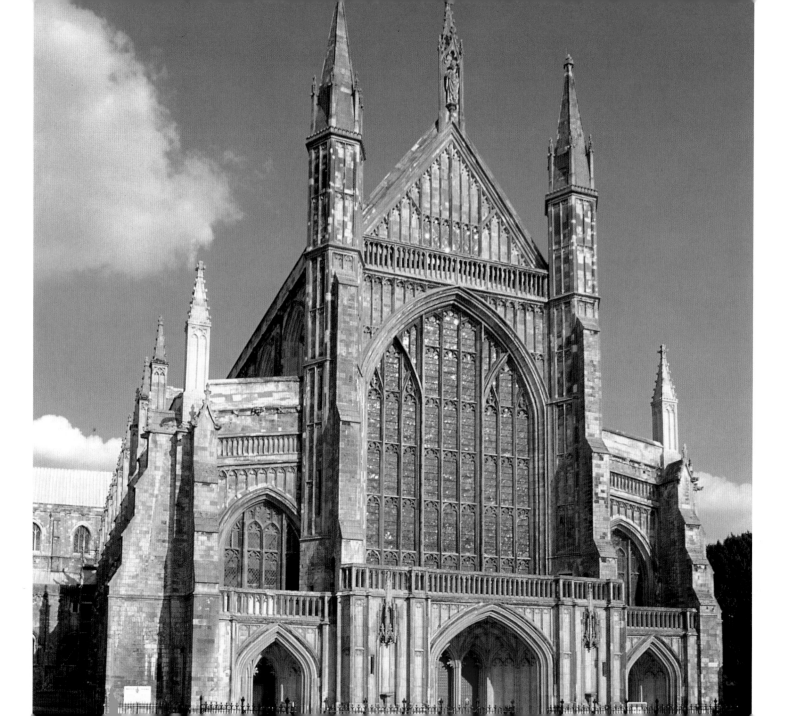

WINCHESTER CATHEDRAL

The first cathedral at Winchester was built in *c.* 645 by the Saxon King Cenwalh and dedicated to St Peter. The present cathedral, just south of the demolished Saxon building, was begun in 1079 by the first Norman Bishop of Winchester, Walkelin. It was consecrated in 1093 and dedicated to St Peter, St Paul and St Swithun, Bishop of Winchester (852-62), whose shrine became a centre of pilgrimage. The transformation from Norman to Gothic was started by William of Edington (1345-66) and continued by William of Wykeham (1367-1404), who was responsible for the Perpendicular arches and vaulting of the nave. Further additions and alterations were carried out over succeeding centuries. At 556 feet from east to west, it is the second longest church in Europe, after St Peter's in Rome. The cathedral was saved from collapse in 1906-11 by the diver William Walker, who with the help of others underpinned the sinking foundations. Among those buried in the cathedral are St Swithun, King Canute, William Rufus, William of Wykeham, Jane Austen, Izaak Walton, and several early kings of Wessex, including Cenwalh, Egbert and Ethelwulf.

WOLVESEY CASTLE WINCHESTER

Built in 1138 by Henry of Blois, Bishop of Winchester, Wolvesey Castle stands to the south-east of Winchester Cathedral on the site of an Anglo-Saxon palace. Incorporated in the building was an earlier stone block of apartments (now known as the West Hall), constructed by Bishop William Giffard in *c.* 1107. The principal residence of the wealthy and powerful bishops of Winchester throughout the Middle Ages, Wolvesey was captured in 1216 by Louis, Pretender to the English throne and son of the French King Philip II. It was retaken the following year. By the seventeenth century, the bishops had virtually abandoned the palace in favour of residences away from Winchester. In the early 1680s Bishop George Morley decided to replace the medieval palace with a new residence in the Baroque style. By 1773 the house was again neglected, and in 1786 it was demolished except for the west wing, which in 1928 once again became the residence of the bishops of Winchester. The remains of the medieval palace – mainly in its twelfth-century form – are in the care of English Heritage.

FULLING MILL
NEW ALRESFORD

When Godfrey de Lucy, Bishop of Winchester, decided to found a town and wool centre at New Alresford in *c.* 1200, he first had to improve the navigation of the Itchen by building a canal, the waters of which were regulated by a great reservoir (Old Alresford Pond), said to have once covered 200 acres. At the head of the canal, a half-mile south of the original village, the bishop laid out a wide market place (Broad Street) with connecting roads to the east, west and north. The parish church of St John the Baptist – near the junction of Broad Street, East Street and West Street – stands on the site of an earlier church, one of three at Alresford mentioned in the Domesday Book of 1086. It was largely rebuilt in the late nineteenth century. Corn and fulling mills on the banks of the River Alre were powered by water from the reservoir. The mill in the photograph dates from the fifteenth century. Because of a fire in 1689, most of the buildings in New Alresford date from the late seventeenth and eighteenth century, including the birthplace in Broad Street of the writer Mary Russell Mitford (1787-1855).

CHURCH-IN-THE-WOOD
BRAMDEAN COMMON

Hidden amid the trees of Bramdean Common is a corrugated-iron church erected in 1883 as a place of worship for the many gypsies who then lived on the common. Known as the Church-in-the-Wood, the building has a small spire and a stained-glass east window. Services are held regularly in the little Romany church between May and October. To the south-east of Bramdean village, near the entrance to Brockwood Park, is a small sarsen stone circle reputedly built in the 1830s by Colonel George Greenwood over the grave of his favourite horse. (Or is the horse buried under the nearby pile of stones?) Greenwood (1799-1875), who lived at Brockwood Park, was himself buried under a sarsen in Hinton Ampner churchyard. Two miles north-west of Bramdean is the site of the Civil War battle of Cheriton, where the Parliamentarians defeated the Royalists for the first time in pitched battle on 29 March 1644. A commemorative stone can be found at a T-junction on the minor road between Cheriton and Bishop's Sutton. Local tradition holds that some of the dead were buried in nearby prehistoric barrows.

SELBORNE
from THE HANGER

'The parish of Selborne lies in the extreme corner of the county of Hampshire', wrote Gilbert White in a letter to the distinguished naturalist, Thomas Pennant (1726-98). 'The high part to the south-west consists of a vast hill of chalk, rising three hundred feet above the village; and is divided into a sheep down, the high wood, and a long hanging wood called the Hanger. The covert of this eminence is altogether beech, the most lovely of all forest trees . . . At the foot of this hill, one stage or step from the uplands, lies the village.' White, born at the vicarage on 18 July 1720, was educated at Oxford and became a curate of various parishes, while he was reluctant to leave his beloved home. For most of his life he lived at the Wakes, almost opposite the Plestor and church, and in 1751 he began to keep a 'Garden Kalendar' and later a 'Naturalist's Journal'. His classic *The Natural History and Antiquities of Selborne* (1789) was based on the careful observations of his surroundings. Eventually appointed curate of Selborne, he died in 1793 and was buried in a simple grave on the north side of St Mary's church.

WHITEWOOL FARM
near EAST MEON

The South Downs Way, running for 99 miles between Winchester and Eastbourne, essentially follows a ridgeway track that was in use long before the arrival of the Romans. All along the route, which weaves across undulating hills of chalk and flint, is evidence of numerous prehistoric settlements and burial mounds. From Winchester to Buriton, near the Hampshire–West Sussex border, the Way covers a distance of 24 miles, passing Chilcomb, Cheesefoot Head, Beacon Hill, Exton, Old Winchester Hill, Whitewool Farm, Salt Hill, HMS Mercury (a naval school), Butser Hill and the 1400-acre Queen Elizabeth Country Park, created in 1953. Among the chalk-loving flowers on the open, turf-topped downs, often grazed by sheep, are salad burnet, rock-rose, wild thyme and a variety of orchids, such as bee and pyramid. Butterflies include the Adonis blue and silver-spotted skipper. The River Meon, rising near South Farm, east of Whitewool Farm, flows north to the village of East Meon before turning west and then south-west to enter the Solent beyond Fareham.

Lyndhurst and the New Forest

LYNDHURST HILL
near EMERY DOWN

In 1826 William Cobbett wrote: 'This New Forest is a piece of property, as much belonging to *the public* as the Custom-House at London is. There is no man, however poor, who has not a right in it. Every man is owner of a part of the deer, the game, and of the money that goes to the keepers; and yet, any man may be *transported*, if he go out by night to catch any part of this game! We are compelled to pay keepers for preserving game to eat up the trees that we are compelled to pay people to plant!' From the exclusive hunting ground of kings to an important timber-producing area to a National Nature Reserve, the function of the New Forest has changed significantly since William the Conqueror created it in around 1079, when he destroyed dwellings and established cruel forest laws to prevent others from hunting royal game. For almost 700 years the forest trees were deciduous hardwoods, mainly beech and oak. Faster-growing softwood conifers were first introduced in the latter half of the eighteenth century. Managed by the Forestry Commission, the area of conifer forest today roughly balances that of broadleaved woodland.

Some thirteen years after the Norman Conquest in 1066, William I created a royal hunting preserve in the south-west corner of Hampshire, changing its name from *Ytene*, 'the furze-covered wasteland', to *Nova Foresta*, or 'New Forest'. 'Forest', however, is misleading, for even then it consisted of high wind-swept heathland, partly wooded scrubland and low-lying marshland. More accurately, the New Forest was largely an area of unarable land, exclusively reserved for the royal recreation of hunting the 'beasts of the forest' (red, fallow and roe deer, as well as wild boar). To protect royal game the king introduced the hated forest law, which not only removed the forest-dwellers' ancient rights but meted out severe and cruel penalties for those who interfered with the beasts (the flesh of which was known as 'venison') or their haunts.

Perhaps it was because of the harshness of his laws that long after his lifetime William was accused of destroying all the towns, villages and churches within the boundaries of his New Forest. 'This he did,' wrote William Camden in *Britannia* (1586), 'either to make a more easy access for his Normans in case there should be a new insurrection in this Island after his supposed Conquest of it; or to indulge himself in hunting; or to raise money by methods though never so unjust. For he, more merciful to beasts than to mankind, appointed a most grievous pecuniary mulct [fine], and other more severe penalties, to be inflicted on those who should trespass on his game.' More recent research (supported by the Domesday records of 1086), however, has established that the devastation was not as great as past historians have claimed. Being relatively infertile with sparsely scattered farms and homesteads, the land could hardly have been a populous agricultural region.

Two of William's sons were killed in the New Forest: Richard was gored to death by a stag, and William Rufus was shot by an arrow. A monument known as the Rufus Stone marks the supposed spot where the 'Red' king fell while hunting on 2 August 1100. There has been much speculation about whether William's death was accidental or deliberate. Some facts seem to suggest a plot by Rufus's brother, Henry, who wasted no time in seizing both the treasury and the throne. It also seems curious that Sir Walter Tyrrell (or Tirel), who loosed the fatal arrow, fled the scene and perhaps even the country. There are few other facts to conclusively support the conspiracy theory. What exactly happened on that fateful day will probably never be known. But such was the dead king's standing in the country, that when the cathedral tower under which he was buried collapsed, the cause was attributed to Rufus and his unworthiness for Christian burial.

During the reign of the Norman kings, the forest was primarily a place of recreation rather than a source of timber. The unrestricted grazing of deer and domestic animals, however, seriously prevented seedlings and young shoots from growing into dense scrub and mature woodland. By the end of the fifteenth century, the demand for timber as the country's main raw material had increased to such an extent that the first tree-growing act was brought into force. It meant that tracts of the forest could be enclosed for growing new trees. Once the woodland was established, the fences were removed and the animals allowed access. Other acts followed, the royal hunting rights became less and less important, and in 1698 an act was passed that gave the Crown the 'rolling power' of afforestation, entitling the foresters the right to enclose an area of woodland up to 6000 acres. Once the trees had matured, the area could be re-opened and another area enclosed and planted. It was a measure that generated a lot of ill-feeling among the inhabitants (Commoners), whose grazing rights (commoning) were increasingly being eroded. Under the Deer Removal Act of 1851 unsuccessful attempts were made to destroy the deer, while yet more land was marked for plantations. Opposition from the Commoners, this time with the support of the public, led to the act of 1877, under which the Crown relinquished its 'rolling power' and was forced to limit planting to previously enclosed areas.

Today most of the New Forest – which covers an area of some 145 square miles – is managed by the Forestry Commission on behalf of the Crown. A mandate presented in 1971 at the Verderers' Court, Lyndhurst, stated: 'The New Forest is to be regarded as a national heritage and priority given to the conservation of its traditional character.' Further objectives include the conservation of the 'Ancient and Ornamental Woodlands' without regard to timber production, the preservation of the existing balance between conifers and broadleaves, the production of sound timber from the Statutory Inclosures, and the accommodation of public recreation. In the same year the medieval forest law was formally abolished by the Wild Creatures and Forest Laws Act.

Six of the ancient benefits of the Commoners, who were prohibited from owning open forest lands, still survive. Known as 'Rights of Common', they are the 'Common of

Pasture', allowing ponies, cattle and donkeys to graze on the open forest; the 'Common of Pannage' or 'Mast', permitting pigs to forage on the autumn crop of acorns and beechnuts; the 'Common of Turbary', to cut turf for fuel; the 'Common of Estovers', to collect firewood; the 'Common of Marl', to dig marl (limy clay) from certain pits as a form of manuring; and the 'Common of Pasture', to graze sheep.

All the commonable animals let loose to graze upon the forest have to be branded with their owner's mark. A complete register of the identification brands is kept by the Verderers, whose job it is to control and administer the Rights of Common. They were originally officers of the Crown, appointed to preserve the royal beasts' habitat, or *vert* (green fodder), from which their name derives. Today, in addition to controlling and administering the Rights of Common, they have the power to veto any development deemed to be detrimental to the forest. The ancient Verderers' Court meets in the late fourteenth-century Verderers' Hall, once situated within or beside the manor house at Lyndhurst, but now part of the nineteenth-century Queen's House, which also contains the Forestry Commission offices. The Verderers, of which there are ten, appoint four Agisters (a name derived from the Old French for 'receiving payment') to oversee the welfare of all the commonable animals in the area of the forest for which they are responsible. Their duties also involve looking after animals that have been injured in road accidents – an occurrence that despite speed restrictions and other preventative measures happens all too regularly.

The Foresters (now employees of the Forestry Commission) look after the day-to-day management of the forest. A thousand years ago their job was to look after the royal game; thus they were referred to as Keepers. They became timber growers when the Navy required New Forest oak to build ships (a warship like the *Agamemnon* required 2000 mature trees). Today they have become managers of a forest that not only caters for timber production but the recreational needs of around eight million tourists annually. The role of policing the forest is the responsibility of the Keepers, who also control the number of deer by culling.

In 1992 the New Forest was given the unofficial status of a National Park. It remains, however, under the control of Verderers, Agisters, Foresters, Keepers and Commoners – time-honoured guardians of the living New Forest.

FURZEY GARDENS
MINSTEAD

Established in 1922, Furzey
Gardens boast a wide collection
of trees and flowering shrubs,
including rhododendron, azaleas,
eucryphias and heathers. Much
of the planting is informal, and
because of its pesticide-free envi-
ronment wild flowers are abundant. The eight-acre gardens are
open to the public. The red-
brick, timber-framed Forest
Cottage is reputed to have been
built in 1560 with wood from the
Lymington shipyards. Like the
adjacent Will Selwood Gallery,
the cottage is thatched with
wheat reed. Furzey House, built
in 1922, is thatched with freshwater reed, while the lakeside shelter is thatched with heather. The
church of All Saints at Minstead
is remarkable for its three-decker
pulpit, upper and lower galleries
and pews, among them three
Georgian 'parlour pews', each
built with its own outside
entrance, fireplace and chimney.
In the churchyard is the grave of
Sir Arthur Conan Doyle (1859-
1930), creator of Sherlock
Holmes. The Trusty Servant inn
has a sign copied from a painting
at Winchester College symboliz-
ing the perfect servant – a man
with a pig's head, ass's ears and
stag's feet. It is copied from a
painting at Winchester College.

RUFUS STONE
CANTERTON GLEN

William II, nicknamed 'Rufus' or
'the Red' because of his ruddy
complexion, was killed on 2
August 1100 while hunting in the
New Forest. Sir Walter Tyrrell,
who loosed the fatal arrow,
apparently fled the country.
Although William's death was
widely held to have been an
accident, some speculated that he
had been assassinated by order
of his younger brother, Henry,
who had promptly seized the
throne. William was taken by cart
to Winchester where he was
buried unceremoniously in the
cathedral. Florence of Worcester
(d. 1118) recorded that during
William's reign 'the sea often
overflowed the shore, drowning
men and cattle, and destroying
many towns and houses; in the
district called Barrucsire
[Berkshire], a short time before
his death, blood flowed from a
fountain for three weeks; and the
devil frequently appeared in the
woods in a horrible form to
many Normans, and spoke with
them much concerning the king'.
The Rufus Stone is said to mark
the site of the oak tree against
which Tyrrell's arrow deflected
before striking the king. The
three-sided stone of 1742 was
encased by a cast-iron pillar
in 1841.

BLACKWATER RHINEFIELD

Blackwater is one of numerous New Forest streams, including the Ober Water and Highland Water, that unite above Bolderford Bridge to form the Lymington River. Its name derives from the dark peat-stained appearance of the water. The photograph was taken near the Rhinefield Ornamental Drive, about three miles south-west of Lyndhurst. Originally a track leading to a hunting lodge in the forest, the drive is lined by a rich species of trees and shrubs, many of which are not native to the forest. The Tall Trees Walk, running parallel to the drive on both sides, was planted in 1859 and now contains some of the tallest conifers in Britain. Among the varieties are a 132-foot Redwood and a pair of giant Wellingtonias, one of which is almost 160 feet tall. The Rhinefield Ornamental Drive continues north across the A35 as the Bolderwood Ornamental Drive. From car parks at the ends of both drives there are waymarked walks through the forest. Rhinefield House, a stone mansion set in attractive grounds, was built in *c*. 1890 and is thought to stand on or near the site of William I's hunting lodge.

PORTUGUESE FIREPLACE
near EMERY DOWN

In the two-square-miles of New Forest south-west of Emery Down are a number of interesting sites, such as the fireplace commemorating the Portuguese Army unit that was camped on the site during World War I while helping the depleted labour force produce timber for the war effort. The fireplace used to be in the cookhouse. Nearby is the Holidays Hill Reptiliary, run by the Forestry Commission, which contains a collection of reptiles and amphibians, including adders, slow-worms, frogs and toads. The Knightwood Oak, in the Monarchs' Grove to the south-west, was planted in *c*. 1600, making it one of the oldest trees in the forest. Also in the grove are eighteen oaks planted in 1979 to honour all the recorded visits to the forest by reigning monarchs from William I to Edward VII. Just outside the grove are The Queen's Oak and The Edinburgh Oak, planted in 1979 and 1988 respectively. At the northern end of the Bolderwood Drive, near the Deer Fields and Observation Platforms, is the Radnor Stone, erected in 1970 to commemorate the 7th Earl of Radnor and which has engravings of wildlife found in the forest.

BEEHIVE COTTAGE
LYNDHURST

Ancient capital and administrative centre of the New Forest, Lyndhurst stands at an important crossroads near the source of the Beaulieu River. It is recorded in the Domesday Book of 1086 as Linhest, meaning 'lime-tree wood'. On the western outskirts of the town at Swan Green are a number of thatched cottages like Beehive Cottage. The parish church of St Michael and All Angels, sited on a large mound, was built in Gothic style during the 1860s and has windows designed by Edward Burne-Jones. A fresco painted by the Pre-Raphaelite Lord Leighton depicts the Parable of the Wise and Foolish Virgins. Alice Hargreaves (née Liddell), who inspired Lewis Carroll's *Alice's Adventures in Wonderland* (1865), is buried in the church-yard. The ancient Verderers' Court, where New Forest laws are administrated, meets in the Verderers' Hall, Queen's House, which also contains the Forestry Commission offices. The hall is open to the public when the court is in session. The New Forest Museum and Visitor Centre offers information on the history, traditions, characters and wildlife of the forest.

THATCHED COTTAGE
BEAULIEU

On his way to the village of Beaulieu in 1826 William Cobbett passed through 'a wood, chiefly of beech, and that beech seemingly destined to grow food for pigs, of which we saw, during this day, many thousands. I should think that we saw at least a hundred hogs to one deer. I stopped, at one time, and count-ed the hogs and pigs just round about me and they amounted to 140, all within 50 or 60 yards of my horse.' Pigs can still be found feeding on acorns and beechmast in the New Forest. But of the 5000 or so commonable animals (ponies, cattle, pigs and a few sheep) turned out to graze, ponies and cattle account for the majority. Beaulieu, French for 'beautiful place', developed across the river from the abbey. Although most of the buildings are of red brick and date from the eighteenth and nineteenth centuries, there are a few thatched structures. A mile south-east of the village, at Bailey's Hard, are the remains of a brick-yard that flourished from the 1790s to the early twentieth century. Bailey's Hard is also noted for being the first shipyard on the Beaulieu River with its construction of the warship *Salisbury* in 1698.

BUCKLER'S HARD
BEAULIEU

Buckler's Hard lies on the west bank of the meandering Beaulieu River. Consisting of a single wide street flanked by two rows of Georgian houses running down towards the beach, the village – formerly called Montagu Town – was created by John, 2nd Duke of Montagu, in the 1720s as a private port for the import of sugar from the West Indies. The port never materialized, but it became a thriving shipbuilding centre, where merchant ships and naval vessels were constructed from local New Forest timber. William Gilpin (1724-1804) remarked critically: 'The large timber yards, houses, and ships on the stocks make a violent chasm in the landscape.' The house in which the master shipbuilder Henry Adams lived from 1749 to 1805 is now a hotel. The chapel of the Blessed Virgin Mary was formerly a cobbler's shop and later a school. A cellar under the floor was once used as a smuggler's den. Among the exhibits in the Maritime Museum are models of ships constructed at the yard, including the 64-gun *Agamemnon* launched in 1781 and mainstay of Nelson's fleet at Trafalgar.

PALACE HOUSE
BEAULIEU

At the tidal limit of the Beaulieu River stands the Palace House, home of the Montagu family since 1538. It was at first the gatehouse to Beaulieu Abbey, founded by King John in 1204 for Cistercian monks. Much of the abbey was robbed and destroyed after the Dissolution, and some of the stone was used to build Hurst Castle on the Solent. All that remains of the abbey church are the foundations, but parts of the cloisters and chapter house have been conserved. The lay brothers' apartments now feature an exhibition on daily life in the abbey, while the refectory serves as the parish church. Inside is a magnificent stone pulpit, described by Arthur Mee as clinging 'to the wall like a swallow's nest beneath the eaves'. Beaulieu is particularly noted for its National Motor Museum, which contains over 250 vehicles and covers almost every aspect of motoring history since 1895. St Leonard's Grange, near the mouth of the river, belonged to the abbey and contains the remains of a massive tithe barn over 216 feet long. The grange, or granary farm, also had its own chapel, the ruins of which still stand.

QUAY STREET
LYMINGTON

Recorded in the Domesday Book as Lentune, Lymington became a self-governing borough in the late twelfth century. A port and shipbuilding centre, the town's principal asset was the 'salterns', or salt-works, on the estuary. When Celia Fiennes visited the town in the late seventeenth century, the trade was at its peak, shipping large quantities of refined salt to London. In 1722 Daniel Defoe noted that apart from salt there was no 'foreign commerce, except it be what we call smuggling, and roguing, which, I may say, is the reigning commerce of all this part of the English coast'. The Lymington smugglers are said to have used subterranean passages to shift the contraband from one house to another. Press-gangs operated from the Harlequin Inn (now Pressgang Cottage) in Bath Road. The Old Customs House in Quay Street, dating from *c.* 1680, is now Hawkes the jewellers. During Victorian times the town became a popular resort. With narrow cobbled lanes, Georgian houses and a church featuring an unusual cupola-topped tower, Lymington is today a busy yachting centre linked to the Isle of Wight by a ferry service.

HURST CASTLE
MILFORD-ON-SEA

Built in 1541-4 by Henry VIII to command the narrow western entrance of the Solent against French coastal invasions, Hurst Castle stands at the tip of a long spit of shingle south of Keyhaven. The fortress was occupied by Parliamentarian forces during the Civil War, and in December 1648 it served as a temporary prison for Charles I after his capture on the Isle of Wight. From Hurst the king was taken for trial to London, where on 30 January 1649 he was beheaded. With its twelve-sided central tower enclosed by a nine-sided curtain wall with three semi-circular bastions, Hurst Castle was extensively altered in the mid-nineteenth century. Two massive wings were added in 1861-75 to house 30 huge guns. Garrisoned during both world wars, the fortress is now in the care of English Heritage. The earliest lighthouse on Hurst was built in 1786; the present white lighthouse dates from 1865, and the red metal light-tower from 1910. The tidal mud-flats stretching north-east to the estuary of the Lymington River form an important nature reserve that supports rare sea plants and a great variety of birds.

Lyme Regis and the Dorset Coast

MAN O' WAR BAY
DURDLE DOOR

One of the many wonders of the Dorset coast, the natural rock arch of Durdle Door is just over a mile west of Lulworth Cove. Formed by the sea gradually eroding a weak spot in the Portland limestone, it is joined to the land by vertical bands of softer rock, such as Purbeck stone, Wealden clay and chalk. Extending from the eastern side of Durdle Door is a line of jagged rocks – remnants of a hard Portland-Purbeck barrier that once stretched across Man o' War Bay towards Dungy Head. The rock that remains is primarily Portland stone. At Bat's Head, to the west, the cliff is pierced by a small hole, which like Durdle Door will eventually become an isolated stack. The 594-mile South-West Coast Path, which runs past Bat's Head and Durdle Door, is one of several long-distance footpaths that start or end in Wessex. Others include the 85-mile Ridgeway and the 99-mile South Downs Way. It was from the cliffs at Durdle Door, on the night of 28 June 1832 that Lieut. Thomas Edward Knight, a Customs Officer, was thrown by smugglers. He died the next day.

The oldest rocks in Dorset date from the Jurassic period – between 213 and 145 million years ago – when the entire area lay under a warm shallow sea, dinosaurs roamed the nearest land, the earliest known birds appeared and huge meat-eating reptiles dominated the water. Marine creatures were abundant, as were hoards of other smaller organisms. When they died, many of the shellfish fell to the sea floor and were covered by sediment. Occasionally, some of the larger sea animals were buried in the same way. Over countless years the sediment hardened to become limestone, sandstone or shale, and the more durable parts of the organisms, such as bones and shells, were preserved as fossils. Spread over millions of years, the subsequent catastrophic movements of the earth's crust – together with the further laying down of sea-floor sedimentary deposits interspersed with volcanic upheavals, tilting, folding and faulting – brought the Jurassic rocks to the surface, where today they are exposed in the unstable cliffs of the Dorset coast. These rich, fossil-bearing rocks occur in the area between Lyme Regis and Lulworth Cove and in a small area around Kimmeridge Bay on the Isle of Purbeck.

The Jurassic cliffs near Lyme Regis and Charmouth are composed of grey-blue limestone (Lias) bands that are sandwiched between dark grey clay and shale, occasionally topped (as at Golden Cap) by a hard mass of Upper Greensand. The cliffs constantly crumble and fall, thereby revealing the fossils trapped within the mud and rock: ammonites – strange, flat, snail-like shells of varying thickness ranging in diameter from a fraction of an inch to well over a yard; belemnites – long bullet-shaped objects that once formed part of a squid-like creature's shell; crinoids, or sea-lilies – animals with feathery tentacles and a long thin stem by which they anchored themselves to the sea floor; gryphaea mollusc shells, or Devil's toenails; and numerous fish, such as the bony-scaled Dapedium and several species of shark.

Perhaps the most celebrated fossil find in the region occurred in 1810, when the first complete ichthyosaur, or 'fish lizard', was discovered in the cliffs. Although Mary Anning, who was born at Lyme Regis in 1799, is popularly credited with the discovery of the eighteen-foot-long skeleton, the person who actually found it was her older brother, Joseph. Mary did, however, help in the excavation. She subsequently attracted the attention of eminent geologists with further major finds, and her name as a fossil collector became internationally famous. In 1824 she found the first complete fossil of a plesiosaur – a long-necked sea reptile – and four years later a rare Dimorphodon, one of the earliest pterosaurs, or flying reptiles.

Jurassic rock is not the only rock along the Dorset coast to preserve the mineral remains of prehistoric life. During the Cretaceous period (145 to 65 million years ago), calcareous plankton multiplied, small mammals and the first true birds appeared, and flowering plants (angiosperms) developed and rapidly spread. Much of Britain was periodically covered by subtropical seas, which deposited more layers of sediment, chiefly chalk. Between the flooding most of the ground was covered by a layer of dirt and soil. Instead of having embedded marine fossils, these 'Dirt Beds' (located in Dorset, east of Lulworth Cove and on the Isles of Purbeck and Portland) contain the fossilized remains of Cretaceous plants and animals that lived on the land: forest trees; cycads, palm-like plants; insects, dragonflies and beetles; and dinosaurs, such as the small carniverous Nuthetes and the even smaller plant-eating Echinodon. In some cases land-living creatures were washed by rivers into the sea to be fossilized in sedimentary deposits.

At the end of the Cretaceous period whole groups of animals and plants mysteriously became extinct. The Tertiary period (between 65 and 2 million years ago) saw the deposition of a further series of marine and freshwater beds – brown clays, muds and sands – which now accounts for much of the rock in east Dorset. There were further earth movements caused by the formation of the Alps. Fossils found within the Tertiary rocks are often surprisingly similar to modern animals and plants.

Towards the end of the Tertiary period there emerged a strange new creature, known as a hominid, from the Latin 'homo', meaning 'man'. It was distinguished from its ape-like ancestors by a larger brain, different teeth and the ability to walk upright on two legs. Over the next few million years this primitive 'man' slowly evolved into *Homo erectus*, then *Homo sapiens*, of which there were several distinct kinds, including the Neanderthals, which died out about 35,000 years ago. They, in turn, were abruptly replaced by *Homo sapiens sapiens*, the ancestors of modern humankind.

Fossils have formed since life began on earth some 3500 million years ago and will continue to form while life exists. Preserved within the crumbling cliffs around Lyme Regis and along the Dorset coast are the extraordinarily diverse remains of plants and animals – some have been revealed, but many more have yet to be discovered.

LYME REGIS
from THE COBB

Confined in a shallow coombe between highly unstable cliffs, Lyme was recorded as a settlement in 774. It became King's Lyme or Lyme Regis in 1284, when Edward I made it a royal borough. During Elizabethan times it was a prosperous Channel port, because it was protected from the full fury of the sea by the Cobb, an artificial harbour and breakwater thought to date from the mid-thirteenth century. In *Lives of the Norths* (1826) Roger North wrote: 'The Cob is a mole built in the sea . . . there is not any one like it in the world . . . for though it is an immense mass of stone . . . no one stone that lies there was ever touched with a tool, or is bedded in any sort of cement; but all, being pebbles of the sea, are piled up, and hold by their bearings only, and the surge plays in and out through the interstices of the stone, in a wonderful manner.' It was not until 1756 that the Cobb was fully joined to the shore, and in Regency times it was clad with Portland stone. The Duke of Monmouth landed with a small army on the stony shore to the west of the Cobb in 1685. His bid for the English crown ended at the battle of Sedgemore.

PRIORY CHURCH CHRISTCHURCH

The original settlement at Christchurch, which became an Anglo-Saxon *burh*, stood on a narrow tongue of land between the rivers Avon and Stour. Its tenth-century name was Tweoxneam (later Twynham), meaning 'the settlement between the waters'. The monastery was first founded in *c.* 1094 on the site of an earlier church. Attempts to build the priory elsewhere, led to the materials being mysteriously removed. In 1150, the secular canons were replaced by Augustinian canons. The 'Great Quire' became the monastic church and the nave the parish church. Eventually, the town changed its name to Christchurch, after the priory and its legend of Christ and the 'Miraculous Beam'. This legend says that, during building, a great beam in the nave roof was cut too short by an unknown carpenter. Overnight, however, it miraculously lengthened. Responsibility fell on the carpenter, believed to be Jesus Christ, who had been helping to build the church. Although many of the monastic buildings were demolished at the Dissolution, the church not only survived but underwent an almost continual succession of alterations and improvements.

PRIORY COTTAGE CHRISTCHURCH

Priory Cottage stands to the west of the Priory Church. To the north are the remains of the Norman motte-and-bailey castle, thought to have been built around 1100 by Richard de Redvers. Only the stone ruins of the keep (standing on the motte, or earthen mound) and the Constable's House (enclosed within the bailey, or defended circuit) survive. Dating from about 1160, the remains of the Norman or Constable's House, with its tall, circular chimney, is a rare survival of twelfth-century domestic architecture. Place Mill, on Christchurch Quay, dates from around 1100 and was built by the canons of the nearby Priory. It was converted from a flour mill into a fulling mill for the preparation of woollen cloth in 1539. Eventually, it was converted back into a flour mill, ceasing operation in 1908. Today the historic building has been restored by Christchurch Council. The mill is unusual in that the millrace, which powers the waterwheel, takes its supply from one river (the Brewhouse Hole on the River Avon) and discharges into another (the River Stour). Both streams are affected by the tide.

COMPTON ACRES POOLE

'Nowhere, perhaps, among all of man's many endeavours, do we more surely see the face of God than in a garden. The genius who conceived The World of Compton Acres, Thomas William Simpson, bequeathed us just such a glimpse of glory' (from the official guide book). Simpson purchased the twelve-and-a-half-acre cliff-top site overlooking Poole Harbour shortly after World War I. In the ensuing years he created out of the rough steep ground not one garden, but a series of separate, independent gardens, each based on a different theme. Due to lack of staff during World War II the gardens were badly neglected.They were restored, however, by J. S. Beard, who bought the property in 1950 after Simpson's death. Two years later, the gardens were opened to the public. Further alterations under subsequent owners have created the present 'Gardens of the World', which include the Heather Dell (shown in the photograph), Roman Garden, Italian Garden, Palm Court, Garden of Memory and the authentic Japanese Garden – with a temple and pagodas designed and built with Japanese expertise.

THE AGGLESTONE STUDLAND

On the wild expanse of heathland west of Studland Bay are the scattered remnants of a layer of iron-impregnated sandstone that once covered the softer sands and clays of the area. The largest of these isolated boulders is the Agglestone, presumably from the Old English word for 'hailstone', suggesting that it had fallen from the sky. Legend says that it was thrown from the Isle of Wight by the Devil, who meant to hit Corfe Castle but misjudged the distance. The stone, perched on a knoll overlooking Studland Bay and distant Bournemouth, used to be more spectacular, standing like an anvil on a narrow base. Unfortunately, it collapsed onto its side in 1970. Part of the large tract of Purbeck heathland owned by the National Trust, which includes the freshwater lagoon called the Little Sea, has been turned into a nature reserve. Among the creatures inhabiting the heather- and gorse-covered landscape are the rare sand lizard and smooth snake, and the secretive Dartford warbler, distinguished from other British warblers in that it does not migrate for the winter.

ROUND ISLAND
from ARNE PENINSULA

From the ancient port of Wareham the rivers Frome and Piddle converge to enter Poole Harbour by way of the Wareham Channel, which sweeps in an arc around the northern tip of the Arne peninsula. Round Island, the southern extension of Long Island, is one of many islands lying within the shelter of Poole Harbour. The largest is Brownsea Island, owned by the National Trust. Covering some 500 acres, it has a long and varied history: an Anglo-Saxon chapel, belonging to Cerne Abbey, was sacked and pillaged by Danish raiders in 1015; during the nineteenth century, the island was extensively mined for china clay; and in August 1907 Robert Baden Powell, founder of the scout and guide movements, chose Brownsea for his first scout camp. Oil has been drilled on Furzey Island since 1985. The first well on the Isle of Purbeck, however, began production at Kimmeridge in 1961. Further exploration in the 1970s revealed a much larger oil field at Wytch Farm, west of Studland Bay. Further finds at Arne, Goathorn and Studland led to Purbeck being dubbed 'Dorset's Texas'.

MILLPOND AND CHURCH SWANAGE

Swanage grew up as a small fishing village at a ferry crossing on the south side of what was once a broad flood plain or lake. Today the site is occupied by the parish church of St Mary and the Millpond, with its bubbling spring and black swans. During medieval times the Purbeck stone trade was centred on Corfe, but after the castle's destruction during the Civil War, the focus of operations shifted east. Swanage became a port, shipping locally quarried building stone to London and elsewhere. The town rapidly expanded. To enforce 'good conduct and regular behaviour', a lock-up, or 'Blind-House', was built in 1802 on the north side of the church; it is now behind the Town Hall. The Stone Quay was built in *c.* 1825. In the latter half of the nineteenth century, many unwanted objects were shipped from London to Swanage as ballast, including lamp-posts, bollards and the front of the Old Mercers' Hall, Cheapside, which now adorns the Town Hall. The transformation of the industrial port into a seaside resort was accelerated by the arrival of the railway in 1885.

VILLAGE AND CASTLE CORFE

Standing on a steep conical hill in a gap between the Purbeck ridge of hills, Corfe Castle's strategic position proved vital in the defence of inland Dorset from sea-borne invasion. Some sort of fortification is believed to have been on the site since Roman times. It was at Corfe on 18 March 978 that King Edward 'the Martyr' was murdered, possibly on the orders of his step-mother, Elfrida, or Elfthryth, so that her own son, Ethelred, could succeed to the English throne. The year after Edward's burial at Wareham, his body was moved to Shaftesbury, where his shrine became an important place of pilgrimage. After the conquest, William I erected a Norman castle on the hill. It seems that his eldest son, Robert, Duke of Normandy, was imprisoned in the keep after his capture at the battle of Tinchebrai in 1106. During the reign of Stephen, when Corfe withstood two assaults, it was said to be 'the most secure of all the English castles' (*Gesta Stephani*). In 1646, just after its capture by the Parliamentarians, the fortress was demolished. The ruins are in the care of the National Trust.

DANCING LEDGE LANGTON MATRAVERS

Stone has been quarried from the South Purbeck Downs probably since Roman times; today the area is riddled with pits and shafts of old quarry workings. Along the coast between Durlston Head and St Aldhelm's or St Alban's Head, the cliff face has been cut back to create ledges and caves from which the Portland-Purbeck limestone was loaded onto waiting ketches. The most easterly of these quarries is Tilly Whim Caves, abandoned in 1812. They are now part of the 261-acre Durlston Country Park, famed for its 40-ton Great Globe, carved from local Portland stone in 1887. Dancing Ledge, so named because it was flat enough to dance on, was a popular landing place for smugglers. Supposedly, they hid their contraband in the roof of Langton Matravers church. One Sunday, however, the ceiling collapsed, bombarding the congregation with 200 kegs of French brandy and killing at least one person and injuring many others. Other popular landing sites included Seacombe and Winspit Quarries, the latter of which closed in the 1950s. On St Aldhelm's Head is a Norman chapel where services are regularly held.

GWYLE COTTAGES TYNEHAM

Towards the end of World War II in 1943, the Ministry of Defence decided to extend their existing firing ranges at Lulworth to include the Tyneham Valley. Just before Christmas on 19 December the inhabitants of the village of Tyneham were forced to evacuate their homes. A note left pinned to the church door read: 'Please treat the church and houses with care. We have given up our homes where many of us have lived for generations to help win the war to keep men free. We will return one day and thank you for treating the village kindly.' Despite a solemn assurance, the villagers were never allowed to return. The houses and cottages are now derelict and in ruin. Gwyle Cottages were built in *c.* 1880, and take their name from the nearby 'gwyle', meaning a wooded valley or gully. The main street, known as Post Office Row, consisted of four cottages: the one nearest the pond being by tradition the home of the shepherd. The head-mistress of the school lived at the other end of the terrace, near the renovated school and parish church (both of which now con-tain exhibitions on the area).

STONE PIER KIMMERIDGE BAY

Kimmeridge Bay has a long industrial history based on the raw materials found in the fossil-rich cliffs, the most important being bituminous shale, known as 'Kimmeridge coal'. It was worked to make bracelets and rings during the Iron Age, while in Roman times the bracelets were turned out by lathes, and the shale was carved to make ornate chair and table legs. It was also used as a fuel, notably around 1618, when there was a glassworks on the site. In the mid-nineteenth century one com-pany held a licence to light the streets of Paris with gas made from Kimmeridge coal. Oil has been produced commercially at Kimmeridge since 1961. The only jetty still visible are the remains of the Stone Pier, built in 1860. Overlooking the bay are the ruins of Clavell Tower, erected in 1830 by John Clavell, the local vicar and squire. Although variously described as a lighthouse, sea-mark, look-out post, folly and even an observatory, it may have been used as a signalling tower by smugglers, who not only fre-quented the bay but landed their contraband at Clavell's Hard to the east.

MUPE AND WORBARROW BAYS
from MUPE ROCKS

Smuggling along the Wessex coast was prevalent until the early nineteenth century, when preventative measures began to take effect. Until then the main occupations of most coastal communities were fishing, farming and smuggling. Not until the 1840s, when Britain adopted a free-trade policy by slashing import and export duties, did smuggling on a large scale come to an end. Midway between Mupe Rocks and Worbarrow Tout is a sheltered gap in the cliffs called Arish Mell. Its small beach was a convenient landing place for smugglers. North of the gap, at Lulworth Castle – owned by the Weld family – it is said that the maidservants warned the smugglers when Revenue Officers were about by signalling with candles from the upper-floor windows. Lulworth 'fair-traders' favoured a cave situated someway down the face of the cliff near the Fossil Forest. The men were lowered down to it by ropes. They also used a cave near the treacherous Mupe Rocks, after carefully clearing a channel to it through the fallen boulders at the foot of the cliffs.

MUPE ROCKS
from FLOWER'S BARROW

High up on Rings Hill above Worbarrow Bay are the earth-work remains of Flower's Barrow, an Iron-Age hill-fort, much of which has fallen into the sea through cliff erosion. Some say that it is haunted by a phantom Roman army. The view south-west from the fortress looks across the chalk cliffs of Arish Mell to the jagged headland of Mupe Rocks. On the horizon is the Isle of Portland, with its naval harbour. The coastal area between Kimmeridge Bay and Lulworth Cove – which includes Mupe, Worbarrow, Brandy and Hobarrow Bays – is used by the army as a firing range and at certain times is closed to the public. Because of the danger of unexploded shells, it is advisable to keep to the designated paths and leave any metallic objects alone. The Bindon Range above Mupe Rocks has been used as a tank firing area since 1916, while the Heath Range north of Whiteway Hill and the Tyneham Valley were taken over during World War II. Like the villagers of Tyneham, the people of Worbarrow Bay were evicted from their homes. Little remains of their fishing hamlet.

STAIR HOLE
WEST LULWORTH

The violent earth movements that created the Alps during the Tertiary mountain-building period also created the folds and buckling that can be clearly seen in the strata around Lulworth Cove. At Stair Hole, known as the 'Lulworth Crumple', the gradual erosive action of sea, wind and rain bored a hole through a weak spot in the harder rocks of the Portland-Purbeck barrier to scoop out part of the softer beds behind. Lulworth Cove is thought to be a later stage of the same process: a place where the advance of the sea inland has been slowed by a wall of fairly resistant chalk, but the water continues to eat into the softer Wealden Clay at the sides. The final stage can be seen in Mupe and Worbarrow Bays, where the hard Portland-Purbeck barrier has been eroded to form one large bay out of two separate coves. Over time Stair Hole and Lulworth Cove will merge similarly.

LULWORTH COVE

The entrance to Lulworth Cove is guarded by two projecting spurs of resistant Portland-Purbeck stone that are sometimes called the 'Pillars of Hercules'. To the east of the cove, on a tilting ledge below the cliffs, lies the fossilized remains of a forest that existed some 135 million years ago. Hollow bowl-shaped hummocks, some almost six feet in diameter, are all that are left of algae that grew around the trunks of the ancient pine- and fern-like trees. The fossilized wood is no longer visible, the last pieces having been removed in Victorian times. At Little Bindon, on the cliff above the forest, is a ruined chapel said to stand close to the site of a monastery founded for Cistercian monks in 1149 and abandoned in 1172. Since the late eighteenth century Lulworth Cove has been a popular tourist spot. Before sailing for Italy on 30 September 1820, the poet John Keats is thought to have spent his last moments on English soil here.

OLD HARBOUR
WEYMOUTH

The twin towns of Weymouth and Melcombe Regis, facing each other across the narrow harbour formed by the estuary of the River Wey, were deliberately laid out in the thirteenth century. However, the harbour is thought to have been in use since Roman times. It was through the port of Melcombe in 1348 that the Black Death is said to have arrived in England. The towns – long-time rivals – were amalgamated into a single borough called Weymouth in 1571. Although the town declined as a port, it became a fashionable sea resort in the later eighteenth century, after Ralph Allen, a Bath businessman, advised King George III that bathing in the sea there would benefit his health. The king, who had suffered a mental breakdown in 1789, did just that and recovered. He thereafter visited the town with the royal family almost every summer until 1811. Each time he bathed, crowds cheered, and a band hidden inside a nearby bathing machine played the National Anthem. With its curving esplanade, colourful harbour, sandy beaches and Georgian houses, the town remains a popular holiday resort today.

PULPIT ROCK
PORTLAND BILL

The bleak and almost treeless Isle of Portland, linked to the mainland by Chesil Beach, has been quarried for its pale limestone for centuries. The stone has been used in such famous buildings as Buckingham Palace and St Paul's Cathedral. Once a great natural arch of rock, Pulpit Rock, at the southernmost tip of the 'island', was formed in 1875 by quarrying. The waters offshore are particularly dangerous, with treacherous currents and hidden rocks. Countless ships have been wrecked in the area. The first lighthouse on Portland Bill was erected in 1716, and today there are three: the Old Higher Lighthouse, converted into a private house; the Old Lower Lighthouse, now a bird observatory and field centre; and the tall lighthouse, built in 1906 and open to the public. Henry VIII built Portland Castle as part of his coastal defences in the 1540s. Currently in the care of English Heritage, it overlooks Portland Harbour and the Royal Naval Base. Below the fifteenth-century remains of Rufus Castle are the ruins of St Andrew's church, with its 'smuggler's graveyard'.

WHITE HORSE OSMINGTON

On the hillside above Osmington is the giant figure of George III riding a horse. Far larger than other white horses (323 feet high and 280 feet long), it was cut in the turf in 1815 to celebrate the king's patronage of Weymouth, which began in 1789. In *The Trumpet Major* (1880), however, Thomas Hardy makes it a memorial of Trafalgar. Towards the end of the eighteenth century, Osmington Mills was the head-quarters of the French smuggler, Pierre Latour. It is said that on one occasion John Tallman, a young Revenue Officer, hid up the chimney of the Smugglers Inn (formerly the Crown and later the Picnic), hoping to avoid a confrontation with Latour. Tipped off by the landlord, the Frenchman pretended that he was cold (despite it being mid-summer) and asked for a fire to be lit. Tallman held out as long as he could, but to roars of laughter he was eventually forced to flee his hiding place. The landscape painter, John Constable (1776-1837) spent his honeymoon at Osmington. About a mile east are the remains of the deserted medieval village of Ringstead.

CHESIL BEACH
from PORTLAND

The unique and massive Chesil Beach is part of an eighteen-mile ridge of shingle that runs from Portland to Bridport in an almost straight line. It is separated from the mainland south-east of Abbotsbury by the Fleet, a sheltered lagoon open to the sea in Portland Harbour. The western part of the Fleet is a wildlife sanctuary encompassing the Abbotsbury Swannery. Chesil Beach is remarkable in that the shingle is graded from one end to the other; the pebbles at the Portland end are larger than those at the Bridport end. In addition, the beach at the Port-land end is steeper, broader and higher than it is near Bridport. Some claim that those familiar with the area could tell where they were on the beach at night by the size of the pebbles – a fact no doubt useful to smugglers. Plundering the cargoes of the many ships wrecked on the beach was also a popular and profitable concern. In 1749, for instance, over 10,000 people turned out to loot the stricken Dutch merchantship *Hope*. In the photograph, Chiswell and Fortuneswell are in the fore-ground, with Portland Harbour beyond.

VILLAGE AND CHAPEL ABBOTSBURY

According to Thomas Gerard (1592-1634) in 'Coker's *Survey of Dorsetshire*', the first church at Abbotsbury was built 'in the very infancy of Christianity amongst the Britons'. Repeatedly pillaged by Saxon sea-raiders, it was finally abandoned in the sixth century and fell into decay. During Anglo-Saxon times Abbotsbury may have been a seasonal pirate stronghold because of its safe anchorage in the Fleet. The Benedictine monastery was probably founded in the 1040s by Orc, the Danish steward of King Canute, and his wife, Thola. As the monastery prospered, becoming one of the wealthiest in Dorset, the village grew in size and importance and was given the right to hold a market by Edward I. It had its own separate parish church (St Nicholas), which, unlike the monastic church (St Peter), survives. Remains of the monastery today include the great Tithe Barn, built around 1400 (originally 270 feet long), and the hill-top ruins of St Catherine's Chapel. The strip lynchets on its slopes are medieval. The village is also famous for its Swannery, founded by monks over 600 years ago.

CHARMOUTH AND LYME REGIS
from GOLDEN CAP

The South-West Coast Path enters Dorset from Devon at the seaside resort of Lyme Regis and threads its way east towards Poole by way of Charmouth and the National Trust's 2000-acre Golden Cap estate. On the western slopes of Golden Cap – the highest cliff on the south coast of England at 618 feet above sea-level – are the ruins of St Gabriel's church, thought to date from the thirteenth century. Together with the nearby row of thatched holiday cottages (formerly a large farmhouse), it is all that remains of the small fishing village of Stanton St Gabriel, the last inhabitants having departed after 1825 when the old coastal road was re-routed. Dating from *c.* 1500, the Queen's Hotel at Charmouth accommodated Catherine of Aragon after her arrival in England in 1501 and Charles II, while he was attempting to escape to France after his defeat at Worcester in 1651. The views from the summit of Golden Cap – topped by golden sandstone, confusingly called Upper Greensand by geologists – extend from Portland Bill in the east to Start Bay in the west.

Dorchester and Dorset

MILTON ABBAS

Between 1771 and 1786 the ancient market town of Milton Abbas was demolished by Joseph Damer, Lord Milton (later Earl of Dorchester) and a new village with a broad grass-verged main street built in the coombe to the south-east. The box-like houses of traditional cob and thatch were divided into either two or four dwellings. In the middle of the street is the church, constructed out of materials from the abbey tithe barn, and, opposite, the Tregonwell almshouses, re-erected on their present site in 1779. Lord Milton had demolished the old village quite simply because he had built a great mansion beside the abbey church and did not want the town on his doorstep. Capability Brown was employed to landscape the grounds, and the valley was flooded to create a lake. All that survives of the monastery founded by Athelstan, King of Wessex, in 938 is the abbey church, now used as a chapel by Milton Abbey School, and the Abbot's Hall, completed in 1498. Nearby, a flight of grass steps leads to the twelfth-century St Catherine's Chapel.

To unify the setting of his 'fictitious chronicles' Thomas Hardy classified them under the title 'The Wessex Novels', and in so doing he breathed new life and meaning into an old Anglo-Saxon word that had almost been forgotten by the middle of the nineteenth century: 'Wessex', a term once relegated to the annals of Dark Age history but now generally understood to represent a loosely defined region of southern England.

Although Hardy's Wessex is 'a province bounded on the north by the Thames, on the south by the English Channel, on the east by a line running from Hayling Island to Windsor Forest, and on the west by the Cornish coast', its core and centre is in Dorset – more specifically, in the area around Dorchester where the novelist and poet spent much of his life. The landscape of Hardy's Wessex was partly real and partly imagined. Some features – like Stonehenge, the River Frome and the Vale of Blackmoor, or Blakemore – were retained under their existing names; other places were thinly disguised under 'fictitious or ancient names': Casterbridge (Dorchester), Shaston (Shaftesbury), King's Bere (Bere Regis), Sherton Abbas (Sherborne), Wintoncester (Winchester), Sandbourne (Bournemouth) and Mellstock (Stinsford). But Hardy was not simply concerned with bringing his characters to life within or through the landscape, he was also committed to recording the customs and events of rural Dorset at the time of his youth, and even earlier – traditions that were in danger of being lost forever because of the dramatic changes in country life brought about by the Industrial Revolution and its aftermath. In his General Preface to the Wessex Edition of 1912 Hardy wrote: 'At the dates represented in the various narrations things were like that in Wessex: the inhabitants lived in certain ways, engaged in certain occupations, kept alive certain customs, just as they are shown doing in these pages.' Even as a novelist, he maintained that historical accuracy was all important. 'Yet I have instituted inquiries to correct tricks of memory, and striven against temptation to exaggerate, in order to preserve for my own satisfaction a fairly true record of a vanishing life.'

Hardy was born on 2 June 1840 in a thatched cottage at Higher Bockhampton, a few miles north-east of Dorchester. The house, which was built in 1800 by his great-grandfather, stood on the fringe of a 'vast tract of unenclosed wild', to which the novelist gave the name 'Egdon Heath':

The face of the heath by its mere complexion added half an hour to the evening; it could in like manner retard the dawn, sadden noon, anticipate the frowning of storms scarcely generated, and intensify the opacity of a moonless midnight to a cause of shaking and dread.

The Return of the Native (1878)

Throughout his childhood Hardy was absorbed and stimulated by the legends and stories related by his elders, the folk songs and music played by his family, and the harsh realities of nineteenth-century life. As a young man he witnessed two public executions. After leaving school, Hardy was articled to the Dorchester church architect, John Hicks, and after completing his apprenticeship in 1862, he found a job in London working for the architect Sir Arthur Blomfield. Five years later he returned to Dorset for health reasons and resumed employment with Hicks. Shortly after, Hardy began to write his first novel, *The Poor Man and the Lady*, the manuscript of which was later destroyed. While working on his second, *Desperate Remedies* (1871), Hardy was sent to St Juliot in Cornwall to supervise the restoration of the church, and it was there that he met Emma Gifford, the rector's sister-in-law, whom he married in 1874. Set on pursuing a literary career, Hardy and his 'West-of-Wessex Girl' lived at several addresses in London and Dorset before moving to Dorchester in 1883. By then he had written numerous poems and over a half-dozen novels, including *Under the Greenwood Tree* and *Far from the Madding Crowd*.

Success from his writings not only gave Hardy the means to become a full-time novelist, it enabled him to design and build a house – about a mile from the centre of Dorchester – which after 1885 was to be his home for the rest of his life. Its name, 'Max Gate', was derived from the fact that the toll-gate nearby was looked after by a keeper called Henry Mack. It was here that he wrote *Tess of the d'Urbervilles* (1891) and *Jude the Obscure* (1896), both of which outraged Victorian sensibilities, as well as angering his wife. Shortly after the publication of *Jude*, Hardy decided to give up writing novels and concentrate on short stories and poetry. In 1914, two years after Emma's death, he married his secretary, Florence Dugdale, 39 years his junior.

When Hardy died on 11 January 1928, nation and family were brought into conflict over the place of his interment. In the end a compromise was reached: his ashes were placed in Westminster Abbey, while his heart was buried in the churchyard of St Michael's at Stinsford – the psalming 'Mellstock' of his 'partly real, partly dream' Wessex.

MEMORIAL SEAT TOLPUDDLE

In 1834 six agricultural labourers from the village of Tolpuddle were sentenced to transportation for seven years, the maximum sentence for swearing an illegal oath. In reality the men were punished for organizing themselves into a trade union, which was not illegal. What was 'unlawful', however, was the oath of loyalty and secrecy that new members were required to take. The men were found guilty. Five were transported to Australia, while the sixth, George Loveless, was sent to Tasmania. Public outrage at the cruelty of the sentences eventually led to the men being given a full and free pardon, but their return to England was delayed for some years. James Hammett, the last man to return, lies buried in Tolpuddle churchyard. In 1934, a century after their fateful trial, the Trades Union Congress built six cottages and a museum in the village in memory of the martyrs: George and James Loveless, Thomas and John Standfield, James Brine and James Hammett. A memorial seat was also erected near the 'Martyrs' Tree', under which the men are said to have gathered for some of their meetings.

TOWN CENTRE
DORCHESTER

Dorchester's history dates back to Roman times, when a small military settlement was established on the southern banks of the River Frome. *Durnovaria*, as it was called, became a thriving city and the tribal centre of the Durotriges, who had ruled much of Dorset before they were forced to surrender to Roman rule. After the withdrawal of the legions in 401, the city deteriorated but was not completely deserted. During the Anglo-Saxon period it became a *burh* with two mints, while after the Conquest it acquired a Norman castle (now demolished). Today Dorchester is the county town of Dorset, supporting a number of industries, including brewing. Beside the porch of St Peter's church is a bronze statue of the Dorset dialect poet, William Barnes, unveiled in 1889. The Corn Exchange and Town Hall was built in 1847-8, and its clocktower (at right) was added in 1864. As the tower is only supported by a tiny pillar, it was expected to fall down and therefore came to be known as 'Galpin's Folly', after the alderman responsible for its erection

HARDY MONUMENT BLACKDOWN

On the summit of Blackdown, near Portesham, is a 72-foot octagonal stone tower that was erected in 1844 to memorialize Vice Admiral Sir Thomas Masterman Hardy (1769-1839), Lord Nelson's flag captain on HMS *Victory* at the battle of Trafalgar in 1805. After Nelson was mortally wounded by an enemy sniper, Hardy attended his dying moments. Other towers in Wessex include the Lansdown Monument near Bath, built for William Beckford in 1825-6; Horton's Tower, north of Wimborne Minster, built by Humphrey Sturt in the early eighteenth century; Cabot's Tower, Bristol, built in 1897; and Alfred's Tower at Stourhead. In the vicinity of the Hardy Monument there is a wealth of prehistoric sites. On Blackdown itself are some ten Bronze Age round barrows. To the east, on Bronkham Hill, is a linear burial ground consisting of over 30 barrows. To the west is the Valley of Stones, source of many of the sarsens used in the megalithic monuments of southern Dorset. To the south, on Portesham Hill, are a stone circle and a Neolithic chambered long barrow, the Hell Stone.

MAIDEN CASTLE

Possibly the most famous Iron Age hill-fort in England, Maiden Castle occupies a prominent saddle-backed site two miles south-west of Dorchester. The ancient fortification dates back to *c.* 3000 BC, when a Neolithic causewayed camp was constructed at the eastern end of the hilltop. Eventually, the place was abandoned and a great 'bank-barrow' – an unchambered long barrow, 1790 feet in length – constructed along the ridge. Excavations in 1937 revealed the grave of a man who had been hacked to pieces, perhaps in some sort of ritual. The Iron Age fort was apparently built in four distinct phases, starting from around 350 BC, when the eastern end of the hill was ringed by a single rampart and ditch. In the second phase, about 250 BC, the fort was almost tripled in size to cover the entire hilltop. Defences were doubled and strengthened in the third phase. In the fourth and final phase, between 100 and 75 BC, the fortifications were remodelled. After the Roman Conquest in AD 43, the fort was abandoned, and by 380 a Romano-British temple and 'priest's house' stood on the site.

PARISH CHURCH BEAMINSTER

Dominating the ancient market town of Beaminster is the magnificent, richly ornamented tower of the church of St Mary, built *c.* 1500. Pevsner considered the 100-foot-high structure 'one of the most spectacular of Dorset, up to the standard of the proudest of Somerset'. It apparently served as a gallows for those who were convicted of joining Monmouth's 'Pitchfork Rebellion' in 1685. The town, which stands at the head of the valley of the River Brit, dates back to at least Anglo-Saxon times. It was granted a market charter in 1284, and from a small agricultural settlement it developed into a prosperous industrial town that manufactured woollen cloth and, later, products from hemp and flax. Other industries included paper-making, printing and metal-working. Destroyed by a series of fires, the last being in 1781, the buildings in the town centre date mainly from the late eighteenth century. At Parnham House, south of the town, are the workshops of John Makepeace, who turns out beautifully crafted wood furniture. The mansion and gardens are open to the public.

FORDE ABBEY

The first Cistercian monastery in England was founded in 1128 at Waverley in Surrey by William Giffard, Bishop of Winchester. Eight years later, Richard Fitz Baldwin de Brioniis established a daughter monastery at Brightley in Devon with about a dozen monks from Waverley. The monks, however, discovered that the site was too barren for their needs, and in 1141 they were given a more fertile location at Forde, on the south bank of the River Axe, by Richard's sister, Adelicia. Forde Abbey prospered. The third abbot, Baldwin, became Archbishop of Canterbury in 1184. The last of the 32 abbots, Thomas Chard, began, in Nikolaus Pevsner's words, to 'build himself a dwelling on a scale to justify the Reformation and the Dissolution'. In 1539, before the princely restoration and rebuilding was finished, the abbey was surrendered to the Crown. For over a century after 1540 the abbey was owned by absentee landlords. Purchased in 1649 by Edmund Prideaux, Attorney-General to Oliver Cromwell, it was transformed into a magnificent country house, now the home of the Roper family. Surrounded by thirty acres of gardens, the house is open to the public.

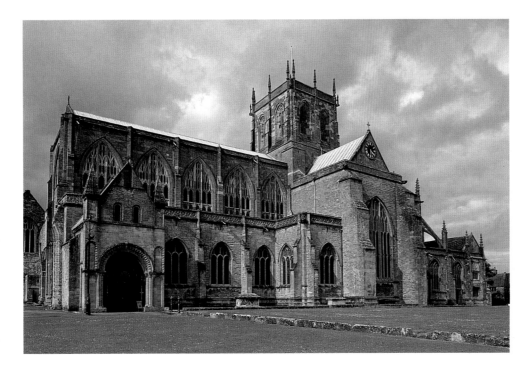

SHERBORNE ABBEY

Situated in the valley of the River Yeo five miles east of Yeovil, the ancient town of Sherborne is noted for its magnificent abbey, public school (founded in the eighth century and refounded in 1550) and two castles (one early twelfth century, the other built by Sir Walter Raleigh in 1594). In 705 Ine, King of Wessex, created the see of Sherborne by dividing the expanding bishopric of Winchester into two. Its first bishop was the great scholar and teacher, Aldhelm, Abbot of Malmesbury, who built a cathedral on the site of the present abbey church. The new see, which stretched west from Selwood to include Dorset, Somerset, Devon and Cornwall, was itself subdivided in 909, and in 1075 it was transferred to Old Sarum. The secular canons were replaced by Benedictine monks in 998. Stephen Harding, a major force in the foundation of the Cistercian Order, was educated at the monastery. After the Dissolution, the abbey church of St Mary – much reconstructed in the fifteenth century – was purchased by the parish. Perhaps its most celebrated feature is its ornate fan-vaulted ceiling.

CHURCH AND EARTHWORK KNOWLTON

Two miles south-west of Wimborne St Giles are the ruins of a Christian church sited in the centre of a pagan shrine. The church dates from Norman times but was extensively remodelled in the fourteenth century. The earthwork – one of three Neolithic henge monuments known as the Knowlton Circles – dates from *c.* 2500 and consists of a rough circle about 350 feet in diameter with two entrances and an internal quarry ditch. To the east is a massive tree-covered round barrow 125 feet in diameter. Knowlton was once an important village, giving its name to an Anglo-Saxon Hundred. It was abandoned after its inhabitants were reputedly wiped out by the plague. Legend says that the church bell was stolen and thrown into the River Stour near Sturminster Marshall: 'Knowlton bell is stole/And thrown into White Mill Hole/Where all the devils in hell/Could never pull up Knowlton bell.' Some say that it was in fact retrieved and placed in the church of either Shapwick or Sturminster Marshall. Others insist that it still lies on the river-bed, never to be removed. The font is in Woodlands parish church.

THE MINSTER WIMBORNE MINSTER

At the confluence of the rivers Stour and Allen is the ancient market town of Wimborne Minster. Around 700 Cuthburga, sister of Ine, King of Wessex, founded a double monastery for both monks and nuns on the site of the present Minster. Cuthburga became abbess of both communities, and her shrine subsequently became an important centre of pilgrimage. After the abbey's destruction by the Danes, it was refounded in 1043 by Edward the Confessor as a college of secular canons. The essentially Norman church, known as a minster and dedicated to St Cuthburga, is all that survives of the collegiate buildings. Composed of contrasting grey and brown stone, the minster has been altered and extended over the centuries. The Norman central tower originally had a spire, but it collapsed in 1600 and was never replaced. The Chained Library, established in 1686, contains about 240 books, the oldest being *Regimen Animarum* (Direction of Souls), a manuscript written on vellum in 1343. The medieval Priest's House, near the Minster, is now a museum.

BRIDGE AND MANOR WOOL

After their wedding Tess and Angel Clare 'drove by the level road along the valley to a distance of a few miles, and, reaching Wellbridge, turned away from the village to the left, and over the great Elizabethan bridge which gives the place half its name. Immediately behind it stood the house wherein they had engaged lodging, whose exterior features are so well known to all travellers through the Froom Valley; once portion of a fine manorial residence, and the property and seat of a d'Urberville, but since its partial demolition a farmhouse.' The bridge and manor described by Hardy in *Tess of the d'Urbervilles* (1891) are on the banks of the River Frome, just outside Wool. In the middle of the bridge is a cast-iron notice that reads: 'Any persons wilfully INJURING any part of this COUNTY BRIDGE will be guilty of FELONY and upon conviction liable to be TRANSPORTED FOR LIFE by the Court.' Like the bridge, the manor dates from the sixteenth century. At Bovington Camp, two miles north-west, is the Tank Museum, boasting 'the largest collection of armoured fighting vehicles in the world'.

ST MARY'S CHURCH PUDDLETOWN

From its source on the hills south of Buckland Newton the River Piddle, or Puddle or Trent, flows south-east for some 24 miles to Wareham before entering the sea through the Wareham Channel and Poole Harbour. Most of the villages and towns on the river's course make use of its name – Piddletrenthide, Piddlehinton, Tolpuddle, Affpuddle, Briantspuddle and Puddletown. Local lore holds that 'Piddle' became 'Puddle' to avoid any embarrassment when giving directions to strangers. Puddletown, a few miles up the valley from Tolpuddle, was substantially rebuilt in the latter half of the nineteenth century, but earlier houses survive around the parish church of St Mary. The oldest part of the present mainly Perpendicular-style church, which stands on the site of an Anglo-Saxon foundation, is a section of the tower thought to date from the late twelfth century. Among the many memorials inside is an alabaster knight in full armour dating from 1471-5. If, as thought, it is an effigy of Sir William Martyn, it was made some 30 years before his death.

HARDY'S COTTAGE
HIGHER BOCKHAMPTON

Novelist and poet Thomas Hardy
was born in a small thatched cottage on the edge of Thorncombe
Wood at Higher or Upper
Bockhampton (Upper Mellstock)
on 2 June 1840. Built in 1800, the
cottage was described – in
Hardy's earliest known poem,
'Domicilium' – by his grandmoth-
er: 'Our house stood quite alone,
and those tall firs/And beeches
were not planted. Snakes and
efts/Swarmed in the summer
days, and nightly bats/Would fly
about our bedrooms. Heathcrop-
pers/Lived on the hills, and were
our only friends; so wild it was
when first we settled here.'
During the early nineteenth century, the cottage stood on an
important smuggling route from
Osmington Mills on the coast to
Sherborne and Yeovil inland. Its
isolated location and distance
from the sea made it a convenient first-stage on the journey.
Hardy, who became an authority
on smuggling, was told by his
grandfather that the cottage could
conceal up to eighty kegs of spir-
its. It is now owned by the
National Trust, as is Clouds
Hill, home of T. E. Lawrence
(Lawrence of Arabia), six miles
to the east.

GIANT
CERNE ABBAS

In addition to white horses, the
turf on the slopes of the Wessex
hillsides has been cut into other
designs, among them a New
Zealand kiwi at Bulford (1918)
and an impressive collection of
regimental badges on Fovant
Down (1916). The only giant to
survive is the 180-foot-high fertili-
ty figure that lies on Giant Hill
above the village of Cerne Abbas,
some seven miles north of
Dorchester. Most experts date the
outline of the naked man to the
Romano-British period, possibly
the first century AD. Brandishing a
120-foot-long knobbed club in
his right hand, the giant is
believed to represent the Roman
god Hercules. A survey carried
out in 1979 revealed a cloak or
lion skin draped over his out-
stretched left arm. His erect
penis, including his testicles, is
thirty feet long, but is thought to
have once been six feet shorter.
Apparently, the navel was
absorbed into the phallus by
scouring in the early twentieth
century. Religious rites connected
with the giant may have been
carried out at the rectangular
earthwork enclosure known as
the Trendle, or Frying Pan,
directly above.

Glastonbury and Somerset

CHEDDAR
from CHEDDAR GORGE

Famous for its cheese, caves and gorge, the village of Cheddar dates from ancient times. Excavations have revealed the remains of a tenth-century palace belonging to the Saxon kings of Wessex. The Market Cross consists of a medieval preaching cross surrounded by a sixteenth-century colonnade. Cheddar cheese has been made in the area since the twelfth century. 'Without all dispute,' wrote Daniel Defoe in *c.* 1724, 'it is the best cheese that England affords, if not, that the whole world affords.' Today 'cheddar' cheese is made all over the world. The spectacular limestone cliffs of Cheddar Gorge are honey-combed with hundreds of caves, including Cox's Cave and Gough's Cave, discovered in 1837 and 1877 respectively. The 9000-year-old skeleton of 'Cheddar Man', found in 1903, is on display in the Gough's Cave Museum, along with flint and bone implements from the Upper Palaeolithic period. Burrington Combe, north of Cheddar, inspired Augustus Toplady to write the hymn *Rock of Ages*. The isolated hill beyond the reservoir is Brent Knoll.

There is something deep and mysterious about the Glastonbury landscape that sets it apart from the rest of Wessex, if not from the whole of England. Unlike Stonehenge, Avebury and countless other prehistoric sites in the region, Glastonbury does not have the dramatic remains of megalithic temples and pagan sanctuaries. It may have the ruins of a once great abbey and the dominant landmark of a tower-topped tor, but they alone cannot account for the vast numbers of people who throng to the area every year. Many are modern-day pilgrims, each seeking to live and experience a more spiritual, holistic way of life in his or her own way. Their search, almost inevitably, draws them to Glastonbury, 'the holiest ground in England', where the earth is reputed to possess special powers, and the landscape is rich in legend and history.

Standing on the summit of the Mendips, overlooking the flooded meadows of the Somerset Levels, where isolated peaks rise through the low-lying mist like islands, the Glastonbury landscape conjures a Tolkienian fantasy world where all things are possible and all kinds of imaginary creatures exist. Indeed, there is much about these celebrated Levels that lends itself to myth. Six thousand years ago, long before the artificial process of draining the land began, these sea-level marshes were a great swamp, with vast expanses of open water formed from the flood plains of a number of ancient rivers. Islands of higher ground, like Glastonbury Tor, the Polden Hills and Brent Knoll, were inhabited by prehistoric people whose only means of contact was by boat or, when the floods receded, by wooden causeways laid down across the reed swamps. The first of these ancient tracks was discovered, probably in 1835, preserved beneath deposits of peat several feet thick. Called 'The Abbot's Way' because its construction was first attributed to monastic builders, it dates from 2500 BC and ran some one-and-a-half miles from Westhay towards Burtle, using an estimated 30,000 alder logs, each about a yard long. An earlier causeway, 6000 years old and therefore the oldest known road in Britain, was uncovered by accident in 1970 by Ray Sweet, a peat cutter. Named in his honour, the Sweet Track ran from near the Polden Hills towards Meare for over a mile.

The reed swamps evolved through fen woodland to raised bog, and after about 300 BC a number of Iron Age settlements were established in the marshlands, notably at Glastonbury and Meare. These lake villages, prone to seasonal flooding, were found in the 1890s and excavated by Arthur Bulleid, who established that the communities grew crops and kept animals.

The Dark Ages followed the Roman Conquest, and by the early Middle Ages historical facts had merged with myths and legends to create out of the silver wetlands a mystical land of dreams and miracles, with Glastonbury – the ancient *Ynys Witrin* or 'Glassy Isle' – at its sacred centre. Here, it was said (and still is said), lies the sleeping Arthur, awaiting his country's call to return. Here is Avalon, 'island of apples', paradise of Celtic legends and abode of the goddess Morgan le Fey. Here is the blessed land of the dead, where the dying Arthur was taken after his final battle and where his grave and that of his queen Guinevere are. Here is the entrance to the underworld, the 'Realm of Annwn' or the 'Court of Intoxication', where fountains flow sweet with wine and where age and sickness are unknown. Here is the final resting place of the Holy Grail, the cup used by Christ at the Last Supper. Here lies the body of Joseph of Arimathea, who visited Britain several times during the first century AD, bringing with him the Grail. Here is the spot where the Christian missionary stuck his staff in the ground, causing it to grow and flower. Here is the site where he built the first Christian church. And here too is the place where he brought the young Jesus, an event that inspired William Blake to ask: 'And did those feet in ancient time/Walk upon England's mountains green?' And here – as Nicholas R. Mann wrote in *The Red and White Springs: the Mysteries of Britain at Glastonbury* (1992) – is 'a place in which systems of geomancy such as "Feng Shui" say the heavenly and earthly currents meet in terrestrial harmony'.

History, however, prefers to rely on verifiable facts. In 878, after being defeated by the Danes at Chippenham, King Alfred retreated into the secret heart of the Levels to regroup his army. Near North Petherton, a few miles north-west of Alfred's hideout on the Isle of Athelney, a gold and enamel jewel was discovered in 1693. Known as the 'Alfred Jewel', it is thought to be the head of an *aestel*, or bookmark, and bears the inscription AELFRED MEC HEHT GEWYRCAN, or 'Alfred had me made'. In 1685 the Duke of Monmouth, the illegitimate son of Charles II, was overcome at Sedgemoor, in what was to be the last formal battle to be fought on English soil.

Yet, in stubborn defiance of logic and reason Glastonbury continues to inspire the imagination. Here, one can be sure, the ancient spirit of the land survives, the earth is sacred, and an indefinable energy can be tapped to heal and revive the weary soul.

DOVECOTE
BRUTON

Isolated on a hilltop above the ancient market town of Bruton is the roofless shell of a four-gabled sixteenth-century dovecote. It is said to have belonged to Bruton priory founded for Benedictine monks in around 1000 and refounded for Augustinian canons in *c.* 1135 by William de Mohun, later Earl of Somerset. The priory was made into an abbey in 1511. After its dissolution in 1539 the lands and buildings were granted to Sir Maurice Berkeley, whose family subsequently gave their name to London's Berkeley Square. The sparse remains of the abbey buildings can be found in the vicinity of King's School, set up as a free grammar school in 1519. In 1540 Leland noted that the stone 'town is much occupied with making of cloth'. The prosperity of the medieval town is reflected in the church of St Mary, distinguished by its splendid fifteenth-century west tower. The River Brue has flooded many times over the centuries, notably on 28 June 1917, when the waters almost reached the door of the church. Since 1984 the town and its ancient pack-horse bridge have been protected by a flood relief scheme.

PRIDDY

The remote and scattered settlement of Priddy was once an important lead mining centre dating back at least to Roman times. The church of St Laurence dates from the thirteenth century and contains a Norman font. On the triangular village green, the thatched stack of hurdles represents 'a symbolic reconstruction of the original collection which was stored here to form the pens for the Sheep Fair which moved from Wells to Priddy in 1348 at the outbreak of the Black Death'. Local lore says that the fair, still held annually in August, will only survive if the hurdles remain on the green. The Priddy Circles, near the Castle of Comfort inn two miles north-east of the village, are according to Pevsner 'the most mysterious antiquities in Britain'. Consisting of a line of four earthen circles, each about 550 feet in diameter, they are believed to be late Neolithic. Among the numerous Bronze-Age barrows in the area are the Priddy Nine Barrows and the Ashen Hill Barrows, both just south of the Priddy Circles.

MENDIP HILLS
from CROOK PEAK

Lying mostly in north Somerset, the Mendip Hills sweep a 23-mile crescent from the Bristol Channel to the Frome Valley. While the 628-foot Crook Peak and the upland village of Shipham are in Somerset, Winscombe – nestling between the two – is in Avon. The highest peak on the limestone range is Black Down, reaching 1067 feet above sea level. Its summit, however, crowned by the Bronze-Age barrows of Beacon Batch, is sandstone. The scattered hill-top settlement of Charterhouse, two miles south-east of Black Down, was an important lead-mining centre during Roman times. Although a road linked the Roman fort to the Fosse Way and Bath, it is thought that some of the silver and lead may have been brought down the Cheddar Gorge to Cheddar and thence via the River Yeo to the Bristol Channel and eventually Rome. Mendip lead was used in lining the Great Bath at Bath and has been found among the ruins of Pompeii. Honeycombed with caves and potholes, the Mendips are a magnet for cavers. The village in the photograph is Winscombe; Shipham can be seen on the distant hillside.

FARLEIGH HUNGERFORD CASTLE

In 1377 Sir Thomas Hungerford fortified the original manor house at Farleigh Hungerford without a royal licence: a serious 'oversight' for which he was pardoned in 1383. His son, Sir Walter – who fought at Agincourt (1415) and like his father was Speaker of the House of Commons – extended the building to enclose the parish church (now St Leonard's chapel). He also built the present parish church, consecrated in 1443, which contains a stained-glass portrait of Sir Thomas. The Hungerfords, who had massive landholdings stretching from Wiltshire to Cornwall, lived at the castle for most of the period between 1370 and 1686. Tales of the wealthy family's evil deeds are rife. Agnes was hanged at Tyburn in 1523, charged with murdering her husband. Walter, her stepson, kept his third wife prisoner in one of the castle towers for three or four years before being executed for treason and unnatural vice in 1540. In the dark crypt beneath the castle chapel are the leaden coffins of six unidentified adults and two children. The castle ruins are now in the care of English Heritage.

NUNNEY CASTLE

The ancient village of Nunney is clustered around a small moated castle built by Sir John de la Mare in 1373. Essentially a fortified tower house, it comprised a tall central block with four large cylindrical towers at each corner. A curtain wall once enclosed the moat on three sides. The strong French influence in its design may be attributed to the fact that Sir John made his fortune from the wars in France. Originally the central block had a steeped pitched roof and the towers conical caps. After a two-day siege in 1645 the castle was captured by the Parliamentarians. They stripped everything from the building, leaving nothing but a floorless shell. Weakened by cannon fire, the north wall eventually collapsed in 1910. The property is now in the care of English Heritage. In the Middle Ages the village flourished on the woollen cloth trade. The Guard House or 'Village Prison' was completed in 1824. The church of All Saints, standing on the site of a Saxon foundation, was heavily restored in Victorian times.

PARISH CHURCH
SHEPTON MALLET

The parish church of St Peter and St Paul is noted for what Pevsner calls 'the most glorious of all the wagon-roofs of England'. Its *c.* 1380 tower, one of the earliest and finest in Somerset, supports the capped stump of a spire that was never completed. Nestling in the foothills of the Mendips, close to the Roman Fosse Way, the market town of Shepton Mallet was an important centre of the wool trade during medieval times – the first part of its name means 'sheep town', the second refers to the Norman family who held the manor after the Conquest. In the eighteenth century it specialized in knitted stockings, most of which were exported to Spain. Today, one of the town's best known products is Babycham. In the Market Place is a 50-foot-high market cross, dating from 1500 but rebuilt in 1841, and also the Shambles, a fifteenth-century market stall. Shepton Mallet hosts two annual agricultural shows: the Mid-Somerset Show and the Royal Bath and West Show.

PARISH CHURCH AND
GENTLE STREET
FROME

In 1724 Daniel Defoe predicted that Frome (or Frome Selwood) was 'very likely to be one of the greatest and wealthiest inland towns in England . . . Its trade is wholly clothing, and the cloths they make are, generally speaking, all conveyed to London'. The population, he noted, numbered 'above ten thousand people', rivalling that of Bath and Salisbury. The fortunes of the town suffered a setback in the nineteenth century when the bulk of cloth manufacture shifted to the north of England. Frome (pronounced Froom) takes its name from the river that meanders through the centre of the ancient market town. The steep and narrow streets and alleys still essentially retain their medieval pattern. Cheap Street has a water-course running down the middle, while Gentle Street is lined with houses dating from the sixteenth to the eighteenth century. On the site of an Anglo-Saxon foundation is the *c.* 1170 parish church of St John the Baptist, which was remodelled over later centuries, culminating in the substantial Victorian restoration of 1852-66.

WEST FRONT
WELLS CATHEDRAL

'Wells is in fact not a city with a cathedral for central feature; it is a cathedral with a little city gathered at the base and forming hardly more than an extension of the spacious close.' So wrote Henry James in 1872. Standing on the site of an Anglo-Saxon cathedral, with an ancestry going back to Roman times, the present building dates from the late twelfth century, with alterations and additions continuing until 1508, when the south cloister was completed. It replaced a Norman cathedral consecrated in 1148. Adorned with hundreds of statues, the west façade is, according to Nikolaus Pevsner, the 'richest receptacle of thirteenth century sculpture in England'. It was badly damaged by Puritans in the seventeenth century but has been restored. The spectacular 'scissor-arches' inside the cathedral were erected soon after the completion of the central tower in 1322 to prevent its collapse through subsidence. The weight-driven astronomical clock in the north transept, thought to date from *c.* 1390, is one of the oldest working clocks in the world and features medieval knights in a tournament.

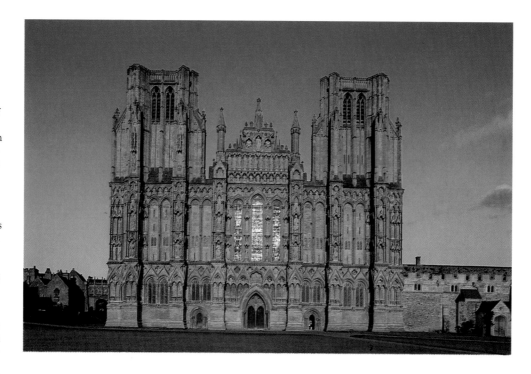

VICARS' CLOSE
WELLS

In 1348 Ralph of Shrewsbury, Bishop of Bath and Wells, formed the College of Vicars Choral (as deputies for the canons they had sung in the cathedral since the 1140s). Now free to marry, their dwellings in the Vicars' Close were completed by 1363. The cobbled street narrows slightly towards the north to increase the sense of perspective. It contains two rows of terraced houses, stopped to the north by a chapel and to the south by the Vicars' Hall. During the early fifteenth century the front gardens and gateways were added. The chapel was altered and given a library above around 1470. Direct access to the cathedral from the Vicars' Hall can be gained by the 1459 Chain Gate. Situated at the foot of the Mendip Hills, the small cathedral city and market town of Wells derives its name from the natural springs (St Andrew's Well) rising in the grounds of the Bishop's Palace. The palace was built in the thirteenth century, while its moat and fortifications were added in 1331 by Ralph of Shrewsbury. Among other buildings of interest are the fifteenth-century Bishop's Barn and St Cuthbert's, the largest parish church in Somerset.

GLASTONBURY ABBEY

Shrouded in legend and mystery, Glastonbury has long been an important pilgrimage centre, laying claim to being the oldest shrine in England. The first church at Glastonbury is believed to have been built in 166 by Christian missionaries from Rome. The monastery is unreliably said to have been established in the fifth or sixth centuries. It was refounded by Ine, King of Wessex, around 688. Enlarged in the eighth century and again in the tenth century by Dunstan, Abbot of Glastonbury and later Archbishop of Canterbury, it became the most powerful and wealthy of all the religious houses in Britain. After Norman reconstruction in 1184, the monastery was almost completely destroyed by fire. Rebuilding began immediately and continued for some 300 years. After its dissolution in 1539 many of the buildings were demolished and the stone used to erect much of the town. The ruins in the photograph are of the choir, transepts and nave of the abbey church. Arthur and Guinevere's tomb site is in the centre of the choir. The isolated lanterned building (at left) is the Abbot's Kitchen.

BURROW MUMP
near ATHELNEY

Forced to retreat from the invading Danes in 878, Alfred the Great, King of Wessex, sought refuge on the Isle of Athelney in the Somerset marshland. Asser (died *c.* 909) described it as 'a spot so surrounded in all directions by waters that save for one bridge there was no access to it except by boat'. Legend says that an Athelney woman, unaware of Alfred's true identity, scolded the king for allowing her cakes to burn. A nearby monument erected in 1801 marks the site of an abbey founded by Alfred in 880 after his victory over the Danes. A mile or so north-east is Burrow Mump, a low conical hill used by Alfred as a defensive stronghold. Later, the Normans built a small castle on the site. The church on the summit, dedicated to St Michael, was once a medieval chapel, and eighteenth-century alterations and extensions were left unfinished. A tablet on the tower serves as a memorial to those who died during World War II. The nine-and-a-half-acre site is in the care of the National Trust.

STEMBRIDGE TOWER MILL HIGH HAM

Before the Somerset Levels were finally drained in the nineteenth century, the hill on which the village of High Ham and Stembridge Tower Mill stands was almost an island. Built in 1822, the Tower Mill is the last remaining thatched windmill in England. It was in operation until 1910 and is now in the care of the National Trust. Like all the windmills of its type, it has a solid fixed tower – in this case built of local limestone – and a moveable cap that carries the sails and turns in the wind. High Ham, with its church and village green, lies about a half-mile north-west of the windmill. The church of St Andrew dates from the fourteenth and fifteenth centuries and is noted for its carved roof, rood screen and humorous gargoyles, which include a trumpeter, fiddler, piper and a monkey nursing a baby. The church at Low Ham, curiously sited in the middle of a field, was begun in *c.* 1623 and, according to Pevsner, is 'one of the most instructive cases of early Gothicism in England'. The remains of a second-century Roman villa, including a large mosaic, was discovered nearby.

PARISH CHURCH SOMERTON

Somerton's parish church of St Michael dates from the early thirteenth century. It was rebuilt in the fourteenth century and further altered in the fifteenth century, when its magnificent nave roof is said to have been carved by the monks of Muchelney Abbey. Although the market town is not alone in its claim to be the ancient capital of Wessex, it was certainly a former capital of Somerset and a fortified centre for the kings of Wessex, including Ine and Aethelheard. Its Anglo-Saxon castle, thought to have stood on the site of the White Hart Inn, was destroyed by the Danes in 877. The shire courts were transferred to Somerton from Ilchester in 1278 – a priviledge that lasted less than a century. Places of interest in the town include: the Town Hall, built around 1600 as a 'market house' in which 'people might stand dry to sell their corn' and in the 'higher house to sell their wool and yarn'; the 1673 Market Cross; the Hext Almshouses, founded in 1626; and The Inn, the oldest of Somerton's many inns, now a private house called 'Cockspurs'.

MUCHELNEY ABBEY

The first monastery at Muchelney is said to have been founded by Ine, King of Wessex, in the seventh century, when it stood on a large island surrounded by marshland. Indeed, the name 'Muchelney' means the 'great island', and even today the village fields are often flooded after heavy rain. During the ninth century the Benedictine house was probably destroyed by the Danes. It was refounded around 950 by Athelstan, King of Wessex, and dedicated to St Peter and St Paul. After the Norman Conquest the abbey was rebuilt. Following its dissolution in 1538, the buildings rapidly fell into decay. The newly built Abbot's House was converted into a private house and the reredorter (latrine block) into a thatched barn. Little else survives. Beside the abbey remains is the parish church of St Peter and St Paul, dating from the early fifteenth century. The nave ceiling depicting bare-breasted angels in period costume was probably painted in the early seventeenth century. Opposite the church entrance is the early-fourteenth-century thatched Priest's House, now owned by the National Trust.

LOCK-UP CASTLE CARY

Built in 1779 as a temporary prison, the Lock-up, or Round House, at Castle Cary is seven feet in diameter with two iron grilles for ventilation and a nail-studded wooden door. Among those locked inside were children, over the age of seven, who played truant from Sunday school. All that remains of the town's Norman castle, besieged and captured by King Stephen in 1138, are earthworks. Excavations in 1890, however, revealed the stone foundations of a substantial keep. Some of the older buildings in the former wool-spinning and weaving town are thought to have been constructed, at least in part, with stone from the castle. The Market House was erected in 1855 to replace a seventeenth-century hall, the columns of which remain. The church of All Saints was largely rebuilt in 1855. Much of the interior was destroyed by the Parliamentarians in 1645. Fleeing from the battle of Worcester in 1651, Charles I – disguised as a servant – lodged overnight at Castle Cary manor, long since demolished. James Woodforde (1740-1803), author of the classic *Diary of a Country Parson*, was born at nearby Ansford.

CADBURY CASTLE SOUTH CADBURY

Of all the sites that have laid claim to being the Camelot of Arthurian legend, Cadbury Castle is by far the best candidate. John Leland identified the hill with Camelot in the 1540s, noting that 'much gold, silver and copper of the Roman coins hath been found there in ploughing; and likewise in the fields in the roots of this hill, with many other antique things . . . There was found *in hominum memoria* a horseshoe of silver at Camelot.' In the mid-1950s fragments of pottery discovered by chance on the hill were found to match similar imported pottery found at Tintagel in Cornwall, another Arthurian site. If nothing else, it proved that the hill was occupied during the period when Arthur was supposed to have existed. Excavations in 1966-70 established that the hill at South Cadbury had been occupied for some 4000 years since Neolithic times (*c.* 3350 BC). There was a settlement on the site in the late Bronze Age, ramparts were built during the Iron Age. Romano-Celtic ruins, possibly once a temple, and a fifth-century timber hall have also been discovered on the site.

LYTES CARY MANOR

Surrounded by a working farm, Lytes Cary is a typical Somerset manor house, taking its name from the Lyte family who occupied the manor from the thirteenth to the eighteenth century. The oldest part of the present building is the chapel, built by Peter Lyte around 1343. Lacking a communicating door, however, access to the chapel can only be gained from the outside. The fifteenth-century Great Hall, contains a copy of the *Niewe Herball*, translated into English by Henry Lyte and published in 1578. The Great Parlour, with its Jacobean panelling, is part of the south wing, dated 1533. Upstairs, the Great Chamber features one of the earliest examples of a coved-and-ribbed plaster ceiling. Commissioned during the reign of Henry VIII, it anticipated by at least twenty years the type of plasterwork usually associated with the Elizabethan period. The Elizabethan-style gardens were created by Sir Walter Jenner, who restored the house and bequeathed it to the National Trust in 1949.

ALMSHOUSES
EAST COKER

In the second poem of his *Four Quartets* (1944), T. S. Eliot (1888-1965) wrote: 'Now the light falls/Across the open field, leaving the deep lane/Shuttered with branches, dark in the afternoon,/Where you lean against a bank while a van passes,/And the deep lane insists on the direction/Into the village.' The village was East Coker, home of the poet's ancestors until they emigrated to America in the seventeenth century. Eliot's ashes were buried in St Michael's church. The first and last line of the poem is carved on his memorial tablet: 'In my beginning is my end . . . In my end is my beginning.' Another memorial in the church is to William Dampier (1652-1715), buccaneer, explorer and navigator, who was born at Hymerford House and wrote books about his travels around the world, such as *New Voyage* (1697). The rescue of Alexander Selkirk, whom Dampier had put ashore on an uninhabited island in 1704, inspired Defoe to write *Robinson Crusoe* (1719). Below the town's church are a row of gabled almshouses founded around 1640 by the Helyar family, who also gave their name to the nearby Helyar Arms pub.

WEST FRONT
MONTACUTE HOUSE

The magnificent Elizabethan mansion at Montacute was designed by William Arnold for Sir Edward Phelips, a successful lawyer who became Speaker of the House of Commons and Master of the Rolls under James I. The Ham Hill–stone building was begun in the 1590s and probably finished in 1601. The east side of the house is adorned with carved statues of the Nine Worthies. In 1786 the main entrance was moved from the east to the west front by Edward Phelips, who added – between the two existing wings – a sixteenth-century porch from Clifton Maybank house in Dorset. The 172-foot Long Gallery on the top floor houses paintings on loan from the National Portrait Gallery. Set in extensive grounds, the house contains fine heraldic glass, rich tapestries and a long plasterwork panel depicting a cuckolded husband 'riding the Skimmington'. The property was given to the National Trust in 1931. Tintinhull House, two miles north, is also owned by the trust. The seventeenth-century house is set in a twentieth-century garden, largely created by Phyllis Reiss, who also helped plant the east court at Montacute.

THE CHANTRY
MONTACUTE

Centred around The Borough –
the medieval market square –
Montacute is built of honey-
brown stone from the neighbour-
ing Ham Hill quarries. In the
Domesday Book, the village is
recorded as *Biscopestone*, or
Bishopston, held by Robert,
Count of Mortain, half-brother of
William the Conqueror, whose
castle – known as Montagud,
from the Latin *mons acutus*,
'pointed hill' – stood to the west.
According to legend, a miraculous stone cross was discovered
on the hill during the reign of
King Canute (1017-35). It was
taken to Waltham, Essex, where
it was placed in a church (later to
become Waltham Abbey). The
tree-covered hill (now called St
Michael's Hill) was also topped
by a chapel. By 1760, when the
present circular stone tower was
built, the chapel had disap-
peared. Montacute vicarage was
the childhood home of the three
literary Powys brothers (John
Cowper, Llewelyn and Theodore
Francis), whose father was the
vicar from 1886. All that remains
of the Cluniac priory is the fifteenth-century gatehouse. A
small road to one side of the
Chantry leads from The Borough
to the entrance of Montacute
House.

PARISH CHURCH
YEOVIL

Dating from the fourteenth century, the parish church of St John
the Baptist was built on the site
of a foundation of which only the
thirteenth-century crypt survives.
Its greatest possession is a
c. 1450 brass lectern. Originally a
Roman settlement beside the
River Yeo, Yeovil was recorded
in the Domesday Book as *Givele.*
A series of disastrous fires in the
fifteenth and seventeenth centuries destroyed many of its old
buildings. Further damage was
caused by air raids in World War
II. Before its rapid expansion
during the seventeenth century,
Yeovil was a small town centred
around the church. In 1630
Thomas Gerard wrote: 'The market, of a little town, is one of the
greatest I have seen . . . the
greatest commodity is cheese,
which being made in great abun-
dance in the adjoining country is
weekly transported hence both
into Wilts and Hampshire in very
great quantity; hemp and linen
are very good chafer [trade] with
them too.' The town's more
recent industries include the
manufacture of gloves, leather, St
Ivel dairy products and Westland
helicopters.

PARISH CHURCH
HINTON ST GEORGE

In 1540, John Leland wrote: 'From Crewkerne by hilly ground but plentiful of corn, grass and elm wood, wherewith most part of all Somersetshire is in hedgerows enclosed, scant a two miles to George Hinton village, so called because the parish church there is dedicated to St George. Here hath Sir Hugh Poulett a right goodly manor place of free stone, with two goodly high towers embattled in the inner court.' The largely Perpendicular-style church contains many monuments to the Pouletts, who lived at Hinton House (Leland's 'goodly manor'). The present house dates from the 1630s. The village is built from the rich golden stone quarried from Ham Hill, near Montacute. On the last Thursday of October the children celebrate 'Punkie Night', a custom dating from medieval times. It seems that returning drunk from a nearby fair the men got lost. Hollowing out mangolds – punkies – the women set candles inside to make lanterns to guide their menfolk home. A rival celebration occurs at nearby Lopen. Both villages claim the custom as their own, accusing the other of stealing it from them.

PARISH CHURCH
CREWKERNE

Largely rebuilt in the Perpendicular style of the fifteenth and early sixteenth centuries, the embattled cruciform church of St Bartholomew at Crewkerne stands on the site of an Anglo-Saxon minster of some importance. Reflecting the prosperity of the town's wool and textile industry, the church is one of the finest medieval churches in the county. An arched niche on the exterior of the south transept contains a unique and puzzling feature – something that appears to be a seat. Speculation that it was once the cell or seat of a recluse or anchorite has recently given way to the suggestion that it may have been a shelf for offerings at some sort of shrine. No one knows for sure. Set in a hollow surrounded by hills, the ancient market town of *Cruche* had a royal mint by the tenth century. Crewkerne means 'the building by a hill called *Cruc.*' Over succeeding centuries it developed a reputation for the manufacture of sailcloth, which it supplied for Nelson's ships and more recently for both English and American racing yachts competing in the America's Cup.

Bristol and Avon

In 1829, at the age of 23, Isambard Kingdom Brunel entered a competition for a bridge over the Avon Gorge. He submitted four designs, all of which involved spans of over 980 feet, his favourite reaching 1160 feet. A modified version of one of Brunel's designs – with a reduced span of 702 feet and Egyptian-style towers – was approved in 1831. Work started in 1836 but had to be abandoned in 1840 through lack of funds. It was finally completed in 1864, five years after Brunel's death, but without the intended ornamentation. In 1885 a woman tried to commit suicide by jumping from the bridge into the River Avon, 245 feet below. She was saved from both death and injury when her petticoats opened and functioned as a parachute. Since 1911, despite a ban, various pilots have been tempted to fly under the bridge, one of whom was killed in 1957 while unofficially flight-testing a Vampire fighter. On the west side of the gorge is a nature reserve. After passing through the spectacular limestone gorge, the River Avon flows for another seven miles before entering the Severn at Avonmouth.

The port of Bristol held a unique position in sixteenth-century England. While the eastern and southern ports facing Europe were largely controlled by foreign merchants, particularly Germans and Italians, Bristol in the west was dominated entirely by the English. The merchants of Bristol, known as 'Merchant Venturers', were a powerful, wealthy and exclusive body of traders. The original meaning of 'Venture' (later to become 'Adventure') was to take a risk, which was exactly what the Merchant Venturers were prepared to do. All merchants, in one sense, were adventurers. The Merchant Venturers, however, were merchants who in their quest for new markets beyond their shores braved the perils of the seas. As Nicholas Breton wrote in *The Good and the Badde* (1616):

> A wealthy merchant is much the heir of adventure, whose hopes hang much upon the wind. Upon a wooden horse he rides through the world, and in a merry gale he makes a path through the seas. He is the discoverer of countries and a finder out of commodities, resolute in his attempts and royal in his expenses. He is the life of traffic and the maintainer of trade . . . By his sea gain he makes his land purchase, and by his knowledge of trade finds the key of treasure.

During the Middle Ages it was the usual practice for traders to band together to form an association that would protect and further their common interests. These associations negotiated terms and conditions while making extremely favourable concessions to their members. The Merchant Venturers of Bristol, for example, were able to use their docks free; those not belonging to their association were charged heavy tolls. By squeezing their competitors out of the market-place they were able to control almost all the import and export of goods through their port.

Bristol is situated at the mouth of the Severn – the great waterway that flows through what was one of the richest agricultural, and later industrial, areas of England. The narrow seven-mile-long Avon gorge protected the port from heavy seas, foreign invasion and attacks by pirates and brought all the advantages of a sheltered, though tidal, harbour. During the twelfth century the port was primarily exporting wool from the Cotswolds, with some trade in leather, corn and cloth. By the end of the fourteenth century, Bristol was second only to London in size and importance. Instead of exporting raw wool, it was converting it into the fine quality cloth for which it became famous. The city prospered and expanded to become one of the leading manufacturing centres of England. Merchandise poured into its market from all over the country. Imports included sherry from Spain and wine from Portugal. Unfortunately, being a major port, Bristol found itself ravaged by the rat-borne plague, known as the Black Death, which swept west from Asia along the trade routes and over the seas in the holds of the merchant's ships. In the summer of 1349, the virulent disease wiped out nearly half of Bristol's population.

The city recovered, however, and towards the end of the fifteenth century, the merchants governed the town and represented it in Parliament. But it was westward, towards the setting sun, that they turned their attention: to the rumours of unknown lands beyond the sea. In 1497 the Italian John Cabot (Giovanni Caboto), together with his son, Sebastian, set sail from Bristol in the *Matthew* and 'discovered' Nova Scotia and Newfoundland, believing them to be part of Asia. In the same year Vasco da Gama of Portugal opened up a route to India around the Cape of Good Hope. Five years earlier the Genoese navigator Christopher Columbus had claimed the New World for his sponsors, Ferdinand and Isabella of Spain. The known world was rapidly expanding, and, realizing the potential, the Merchant Venturers of Bristol were eager to take advantage of the opportunities it presented.

In the late seventeenth and eighteenth century, the city prospered on the slave-trade between West Africa and America. It also benefited from the import of tobacco, sugar and cocoa – commodities that formed the basis of Bristol's manufacturing industries. After the abolition of slavery in the nineteenth century, the port lost much of its trade to Liverpool. The decline and eventual closure of the city docks was brought about by the opening of docks at Avonmouth and Portishead.

Today, there are some who maintain that the Merchant Venturers of Bristol may have known of the existence of the New World before Columbus. After all, they had been to Iceland and Greenland before Cabot's epic voyage to Nova Scotia. That there was a land further west may have come as no surprise to them. It is further claimed that it was a Bristol merchant, Richard Ameryck, a friend and financial backer of Cabot, who gave his name to America – thereby linking the Old World, irrevocably, with the New.

STONE CIRCLE STANTON DREW

On the southern side of the River Chew in the fields east of the village of Stanton Drew are a group of prehistoric monuments considered to be among the finest in Wessex. Consisting of three stone circles with avenues extending from them, they are around 4000 years old (dating from the late Neolithic period) and were probably erected for religious or ceremonial purposes. The largest measures about 368 feet in diameter and originally contained some 30 or more stones, of which 27 still survive. The north-eastern circle is about 97 feet in diameter, while the south-western circle is about 145 feet in diameter. Across the river and under a chestnut tree near Quoit Farm is a stone called Hauteville's Quoit. Legend says that it was thrown there by the legendary Sir John de Hauteville, who was reputed to possess super-human strength. There is a monument to him in nearby Chew Magna church. At the northern entrance to Stanton Drew is the hexagonal Round House, with its conical thatched roof. Used first a lookout tower, it later became a toll-house.

ST AUGUSTINE'S REACH BRISTOL

At the confluence of the rivers Avon and Frome, some seven miles upriver from the mouth of the Severn (Avonmouth), lies the port of Bristol, whose history goes back to Saxon times. In 1247 the Frome was diverted to create a harbour, and during the Middle Ages Bristol became one of the most important ports in England. In 1809 a new floating, or tideless, harbour was built by diverting the waters of the Avon and Frome. After the establishment of docks at Avonmouth in 1877, the city docks went into decline and were finally closed to commercial shipping in 1976. Bristol was heavily bombed during World War II, and many old buildings were destroyed. The church of St Stephen (seen in the photograph) dates from 1440. The church of St Mary Redcliffe was described by Elizabeth I as 'the fairest, goodliest and most famous parish church in the kingdom'. In the Great Western Dry Dock is the SS *Great Britain*, designed by Brunel and launched in 1843. Entry is through the Maritime Heritage Centre.

SEVERN ROAD BRIDGE
from BEACHLEY

The Severn Road Bridge, which links England with south Wales and was designed by Sir Gilbert Roberts, opened in 1966. Stretching 3240 feet between the Beachley peninsula and Aust, it replaced an ancient ferry crossing known in Roman times as the *Trajectus Augusti* and later as the Old Passage. (The New Passage was some three miles further downstream by the Severn Railway Tunnel, completed in 1886.) Defoe visited the 'dirty little village' of Aust in around 1670 and found the sea 'so broad, the fame of the bore of the tide so formidable . . . the water so rough, and which was worse, the boats to carry over both man and horse . . . so very mean, that in short none of us cared to venture'. An anonymous account of a great flood in 1607 records that 'Oxen in great numbers were carried away with the stream, and looked like so many whales in the sea . . . An infant likewise was found swimming in a cradle . . . Nay, which is more strange, conies [rabbits] in great numbers being driven out of their burrows by the tide, were seen to sit for safety on the backs of sheep, as they swam up and down and at last were drowned with them.'

BLAISE HAMLET
HENBURY

Considered by Pevsner to be the '*ne plus ultra* of picturesque layout and design', Blaise Hamlet was created by the Bristol banker John Scandrett Harford to house his retired employees. After purchasing the Blaise Hamlet estate in 1789, Harford commissioned William Paty to build a house and Humphry Repton to redesign the park. The Gothic folly known as Blaise Castle was designed by Robert Mylne in 1766. The estate village of Blaise Hamlet, built in 1810-11 and designed by John Nash, consists of nine cottages set around an undulating green that contains a tall sundial erected in 1815. All the cottages are unique, each with a small garden, an outside bench and doors facing in various directions to discourage noise and gossip among the residents. The thatched Circular Cottage and the tiled Sweet Briar Cottage are shown in the photograph. Like the others they have ornate chimneys of varying designs. After praising the village, Pevsner remarks that it 'is indeed responsible for some of the worst sentimentalities of England'. Blaise Hamlet is four miles north of Bristol city centre.

BATH
from ALEXANDRA PARK

Long before the arrival of the Romans in the first century AD, hot natural mineral springs bubbled out of the ground beside the River Avon. Realizing the therapeutic properties of the waters, the Romans built a town, *Aquae Sulis*, with elaborate baths and a temple dedicated to an amalgamated deity Sulis-Minerva: the Celtic goddess of the springs and the Roman goddess of healing. The town grew to become a major cult centre famed throughout the Empire for its healing waters – which, incidentally, still gush out of the ground to feed the Great Bath at a steady 250,000 gallons a day and a constant temperature of 49°C. After the Roman buildings had fallen into ruin in the seventh century, the Anglo-Saxons founded a monastery by the springs. The present abbey church was begun in 1499 by Bishop Oliver King, whose dream of angels climbing up and down a ladder to heaven is commemorated on the west façade. Today the 'golden city' of Bath, built of local limestone, contains a wealth of Georgian architecture, such as the Circus and Royal Crescent designed by John Wood the Elder and Younger respectively.

WELLOW

The ancient village of Wellow, located some four miles south of Bath, contains a medieval pack-horse bridge, a watermill (now a private house), a circular thatched dovecote and a holy well, reputedly haunted. The ashlar-faced church of St Julian, thought to date from 1372, contains medieval wall-paintings representing Christ and the apostles. Sir Thomas Hungerford, whose family occupied the town manor from 1369, was the first spokes-man for the House of Commons to hold the title of Speaker, taking office in 1377. Less than a mile south-west of the village is the Stoney Littleton Long Barrow, over 100 feet long and 54 feet wide. A Neolithic tomb, it was used for collective burial from *c.* 2000 BC. According to a stone tablet at the site, it was 'declared by competent judges to be the most perfect specimen of Celtic antiquity still existing in Great Britain' after it was restored in 1858. The central gallery is over 40 feet long, with three pairs of side chambers and an end chamber. On one of the entrance uprights is an ammonite cast.

THE COVE
STANTON DREW

Tradition holds that the great stone circles at Stanton Drew represent a wedding party who were celebrating on a Saturday night and were turned to stone for refusing to stop dancing when Sunday morning came. The three stones of the Cove, behind the Druids Arms inn and near the thirteenth-century church of St Mary the Virgin, are reputed to be the bride, bridegroom and parson. William Stukeley, the antiquarian, wrote in 1743: 'Other circles are said to be the company dancing; and a separate parcel of stones standing a little from the rest are called the Fiddlers, or the Band of Music.' The village of Stanton Drew is named after 'Stanton', meaning 'stone settle-ment', and the Drew, or Drogo, family who held the manor in the thirteenth century. The bridge, which spans the River Chew, dates from the fourteenth century. Two miles north, on Maes Knoll, are the earthwork remains of a hill-fort. Stretching some 40 miles from Maes Knoll east to Marlborough, south of Swindon, are the remains of the great earthen wall of Wansdyke. Although its date is uncertain, it was used in the sixth century by Romano-Britons as a defence against Saxon attacks.

Photographic Notes

'Well let's hope the good people of Wessex don't find out the cause of the terrible weather about to come their way!' commented my partner, Sheila, as I set off south to start this book. She wasn't being flippant. As I travelled around the country taking photographs, freak weather seemed to dog my every step.

The Cotswolds, my first book in the Weidenfeld Country Series, brought snow, cutting off whole villages and making the National news. For *The English Lakes*, it was distant peaks capped by cloud. Often I would drive from the Midlands under the most perfect blue sky, with the radio promising a beautiful sunny day. But, by the time I'd reached the Lakes, everything had changed for the worst. *The Yorkshire Moors and Dales*, if nothing else, provided variety. Snow that cut off the roads, making it impossible for even the snow-ploughs to get through. Sunshine and showers: showers wherever I happened to be; sunshine, everywhere else. With *The Heart of England*, at least I was given a chance to fight back and try and confuse my weather-Jonah. Living centrally within the region, I was able to pop out at a moment's notice to take shots when the weather was right. Even so, the elements did their very best to thwart my endeavours. I could almost have sworn that the clouds were racing me to each location! *The West Country* introduced a new element: fog, fog and more fog. Local fishermen scratched their heads and said they had never known anything like it. The fog horn droned on day and night for two whole weeks before any kind of feature appeared in the landscape.

And so to Wessex, a region known for its mysterious and mystical landscapes. At first, I'd thought the gods were smiling on me. Or was it the influence of my name-sake, William Henry Fox Talbot, a fellow snapper, who'd processed all his own pics and had produced some pretty fine photos to boot? Whatever the reason, the weather couldn't have been better: stormy at Stonehenge; glorious at Glastonbury; lovely at Lacock; and wild at Westbury. It was incredible. The first half of the book completed in record time! Thereafter, the freak weather returned with a vengeance. Storms. Lightning. Hailstones . . . It was back to waiting. Oh, what I would give for a sunshine filter!

Technically speaking, I used a Nikon 35mm system with F3 body and 24mm, 28mm, 35mm, 85mm and 180mm lenses; and a Mamiya 6 body with 50mm, 75mm and 150mm lenses. The film was Fuji Velvia.

Rob Talbot

Selected Properties and Regional Offices

ENGLISH HERITAGE

All English Heritage properties, except where specified, are open from April to the end of September every day from 10 am to 6 pm (summer season); from October to March, opening times are Tuesdays to Sundays, from 10 am to 4 pm. The properties are closed on 24, 25 and 26 December and 1 January.

Head Office
Keysign House
429 Oxford Street
London W1R 2HD
Tel: (071) 973 3000

South-West Regional Information Office
7-8 King Street
Bristol BS1 4EQ
Tel: (0272) 750700

South-East Regional Information Office
1 High Street
Tonbridge
Kent TN9 1SG
Tel: (0732) 778000

Avebury Museum
Avebury
Wiltshire SNH 1RF
Tel: (06723) 250
Open all year, plus Mondays in winter

Bishop's Waltham Palace
Bishop's Waltham
Hampshire SO32 1DH
Tel: (0489) 892460

Calshot Castle
near Fawley
Hampshire SO4 1BR
Tel: (0703) 892023
Open summer season only

Farleigh Hungerford Castle
Farleigh Hungerford
Somerset BA3 6RS
Tel: (0225) 754026

Fort Brockhurst
Gunner's Way
Elson
Hampshire PO12 4DS
Tel: (0705) 581059

Hurst Castle
near Keyhaven
Hampshire PO41 0PB
Tel: (0590) 642344
Open summer season, daily; winter, weekends only

Medieval Merchant's House
58 French Street
Southampton
Hampshire SO1 0AT
Tel: (0703) 221503

Muchelney Abbey
Muchelney
Somerset TA10 0DQ
Tel: (0458) 250664
Open summer season only

Netley Abbey
Netley
Hampshire SO3 5FB
Tel: (0703) 453076
Open summer season, daily; winter, weekends only

Old Sarum
Salisbury
Wiltshire SP1 3SD
Tel: (0722) 335398
Open all year, plus Mondays in winter

Old Wardour Castle
Tisbury
Wiltshire SP3 6RP
Tel: (0747) 870487
Open summer season, daily; winter, weekends

Portchester Castle
Portchester
Hampshire PO16 9QW
Tel: (0705) 378291

Portland Castle
Portland
Dorset DT5 AX
Tel: (0305) 820539
Open summer season only

Sherborne Old Castle
Sherborne
Dorset DT9 3SA
Tel: (0935) 812730
Open all year

Stanton Drew Circles
Stanton Drew
Avon
Open all year, except on Sundays

Stonehenge
Amesbury
Wiltshire ST4 7DE
Tel: (0980) 623108
Open all year, plus Mondays in winter.

Wolvesey: Old Bishop's Palace
Winchester
Hampshire S023 9NB
Tel: (0962) 54766
Open summer season only

NATIONAL TRUST

Wessex Regional Office
Eastleigh Court
Bishopstrow
Warminster
Wiltshire BA12 9HW
Tel: (0985) 847777

Southern Regional Office
Polesden Lacy
Dorking
Surrey RH5 6BD
Tel: (0372) 453401

Avebury Manor
near Marlborough
Wiltshire SN8 1RF
Tel: (06723) 388 (answerphone)
Open: house (phone for details); garden, April to end October, Tuesdays, Wednesdays, Fridays to Sundays, Bank Holiday Mondays

Brownsea Island
Poole Harbour
Dorset BH15 1EE
Tel: (0202) 707744
Open April to mid-October, daily

Clevedon Court
Clevedon
Avon BS21 6QU
Tel: (0275) 872257
Open April to end September, Wednesdays, Thursdays, Sundays and Bank Holiday Mondays

Clouds Hill
Wareham
Dorset BH20 7NQ
Open April to end October, Wednesdays to Fridays, Sundays and Bank Holiday Mondays

Corfe Castle
Wareham
Dorset BH20 5EZ
Tel: (0929) 481294
Open mid-February to end October, daily; November to February, Saturdays and Sundays

The Courts
Holt
near Trowbridge
Wiltshire BA14 6RR
Tel: (0225) 782340
Garden only open, April to end October, Sundays to Fridays

Great Chalfield Manor
near Melksham
Wiltshire SN12 8NJ

Tel: (0985) 847777 (Regional Office)
Open April to end October, Tuesdays to Thursdays

Hardy's Cottage
Higher Bockhampton
near Dorchester
Dorset DT2 8QJ
Tel: (0305) 262366
Open April to end October, Fridays to Wednesdays

Hinton Ampner
Bramdean
near Alresford
Hampshire SO24 0LA
Tel: (0962) 771305
Open April to end September; house, Tuesdays and Wednesdays, and also Saturdays and Sundays in August; garden, Saturdays, Sundays, Tuesdays, Wednesdays, Good Friday and Bank Holiday Mondays

Kingston Lacy
Wimborne Minster
Dorset BH21 4EA
Tel: (0202) 883402
House open April to end October, Saturdays to Wednesdays; gardens, as house, but also November and December, weekends

Lacock Abbey
near Chippenham
Wiltshire SN15 2LG
Tel: (0249) 730227
Open April to end October; house, Wednesdays to Mondays; cloisters and grounds, daily

Lacock: Fox Talbot Museum
near Chippenham
Wiltshire SN15 2LG
Tel: (0249) 730459
Open April to end October, daily; closed Good Friday

Selected Properties and Regional Offices

Lyte's Cary Manor
Charlton Mackrell
Somerton
Somerset TA11 7HU
Tel: (0985) 847777 (Regional Office)
Open April to end October, Mondays,
Wednesdays and Saturdays.

Mompesson House
The Close
Salisbury
Wiltshire SP1 2EL
Tel: (0722) 335659
Open April to end October, Saturdays
to Wednesdays

Montacute House
Montacute
Somerset
TA15 6XP
Tel: (0935) 823289
House open April to end October,
Wednesdays to Mondays; garden
and park, Wednesdays to Mondays,
all year

Mottisfont Abbey & Garden
enquiries to:
Mottisfont
near Romsey
Hampshire SO51 0LP
Tel: (0794) 341220 (opening hours
only)
Open April to end October; house,
Tuesdays, Wednesdays and Sundays;
garden, Saturdays to Wednesdays

Priest's House
Muchelney
Langport
Somerset TA10 9DQ
Open April to end September,
Sundays and Mondays

Stembridge Tower Mill
High Ham
Langport
Somerset TA10 9DJ
Tel: (0458) 250818

Open April to end September,
Sundays, Mondays and Wednesdays

Stourhead
Stourton
Warminster
Wiltshire BA12 6QH
Tel: (0747) 840348
House open April to end October,
Saturdays to Wednesdays; garden,
daily all year; King Alfred's Tower,
April to end October, Saturdays,
Sundays, Tuesdays to Thursdays,
Good Friday and Bank Holiday
Mondays

Tintinhull House Garden
Tintinhull
near Yeovil
Somerset BA22 9PZ
Tel: (0985) 847777 (Regional Office)
Open April to end September,
Tuesdays to Thursdays, Saturdays,
Sundays and Bank Holiday Mondays

The Vyne
Sherborne St John
Basingstoke
Hampshire RG26 5DX
Tel: (0256) 881337
Open end March to end October,
Tuesdays to Thursdays, Saturdays,
Sundays, Good Friday, Bank Holiday
Mondays (but closed Tuesdays follow-
ing); grounds only, weekends in
March and October

Winchester City Mill
Bridge Street
Winchester
Hampshire SO23 8EJ
Tel: (0962) 870057
Open April to end September daily,
Bank Holiday Mondays, and
Saturdays and Sundays in October

MISCELLANEOUS

Beaulieu: National Motor Museum,
Palace House Gardens, Abbey
John Montagu Building
Beaulieu
Hampshire SO42 72N
Tel: (0590) 612345/612123
All facilities open daily (except
Christmas)

Bovington Tank Museum
Bovington Camp
near Wareham
Dorset BH20 6JG
Tel: (0929) 403329/403463
or 463953 (answerphone)
Open daily (except 10 days at
Christmas)

Broadlands
Romsey
Hampshire SO51 92D
Tel: (0794) 516878
Open Easter to end September, daily;
closed Fridays (except Good Friday
and in August)

Cheddar Show Caves
Cheddar Gorge
Somerset BS27 3QF
Tel: (0934) 742343
Open daily (except 24 and 25
December)

Compton Acres
Canford Cliffs Road
Poole
Dorset BH13 7ES
Tel: (0202) 700778
Open March to end October, daily

Forde Abbey
near Chard
Dorset TA20 4LU
Tel: (0460) 20231
Abbey open April to end October,
Wednesday, Sunday and Bank
Holidays; gardens, daily all year

Furzey Gardens
Minstead
near Lyndhurst
Hampshire
Tel: (0703) 812464
Open daily (except Christmas and
Boxing Day)

Glastonbury Abbey
Glastonbury
Somerset BA6 9EL
Tel: (0458) 832267
Open daily (except Christmas Day)

Highclere Castle
The Estate Office
Highclere Park
near Newbury
Berkshire RG15 9RN
Tel: (0635) 253210
Open July to September, Wednesdays
to Sundays, and Easter, May and
August Bank Holidays

Jane Austen's House
Chawton
Alton
Hampshire GU34 1SD
Tel: (0420) 83262
Open April to October, daily;
November, December, March,
Wednesdays to Sundays; January
and February, Saturdays and
Sundays.

Longleat
The Estate Office
Warminster
Wiltshire BA12 7NW
Tel: (0985) 844400
House open daily (except Christmas);
safari park, Easter to end October

**Gilbert White's House, Garden
and Oates Museum**
'The Wakes'
Selborne
near Alton
Hampshire GU34 3JH

Tel: (0420) 50275
Open March to end October, daily

Parnham House
Beaminster
Dorset DT8 3NA
Tel: (0308) 862204
Open April to end October, Wednes-
days, Sundays and Bank Holidays

Sherborne Castle
Digby Estate Office
9 Cheap Street
Sherborne D79 3PY
Dorset
Tel: (0935) 813182
Open Easter to end September,
Thursdays, Saturdays, Sundays and
Bank Holiday Mondays.

Wells: Bishop's Palace
Palace Trustees
Wells
Somerset BA5 2PD
Tel (0749) 672341
Open Easter to end October,
Thursdays, Sundays and Bank
Holiday Mondays; August, daily

Wilton House
Wilton
Salisbury
Wiltshire SP2 0BJ
Tel: (0722) 743115
Open daily throughout the year

Wookey Hole Caves
Wells
Somerset BA5 1BB
Tel: (0749) 672243
Open daily throughout the year
(except mid-December to Christmas)

Selected Bibliography

Adkins, Lesley and Roy, *A Field Guide to Somerset Archaeology*, Dovecote Press, Wimborne, 1992

Alcock, Leslie, *By South Cadbury is that Camelot*, Thames and Hudson, London, 1972

Aston, Michael and Burrow, Ian, (eds.), *The Archaeology of Somerset*, Somerset County Council, Bridgwater, 1982

Aubrey, John, *Monumenta Britannica* (compiled 1665-93), Dorset Publishing Company, Sherborne, 1980 (1st pub.)

Beresford, Maurice, *New Towns of the Middle Ages*, Sutton, Gloucester, 1988

Bond, Lilian, *Tyneham: A Lost Heritage*, Dovecote Press, 1984

Bulleid, Arthur, *The Lake-Villages of Somerset*, Glastonbury Antiquarian Society, 1924

Camden, William, *Britannia*, Gibson, Oxford, 1695

Chandler, John, *The Vale of Pewsey*, Ex Libris Press, Bradford-on-Avon, 1991

Cobbett, William, *Rural Rides*, Penguin, Harmondsworth, 1967

Defoe, Daniel, *A Tour Through the Whole Island of Great Britain*, Penguin, Harmondsworth, 1971

Draper, Jo, *Dorset: The Complete Guide*, Dovecote Press, Wimborne, 1986

Draper, Jo, *Hampshire: The Complete Guide*, Dovecote Press, Wimborne, 1990

Dyer, James, *Southern England: An Archaeological Guide*, Faber, London, 1973

Edlin, H. L., *New Forest*, H.M.S.O., London, 1951

Edwards, Anne-Marie, *In the Steps of Jane Austen*, Countryside Books, Newbury, 1979

Fiennes, Celia, *The Journeys of Celia Fiennes* (ed. Christopher Morris), Cresset, London, 1947

Fox, Aileen, *South West England 3,500 BC-AD 600*, David & Charles, Newton Abbot, 1964

Gerard, Thomas, *Coker's Survey of Dorsetshire* (1st pub. under name John Coker in 1732), 2nd ed. Dorset Publishing, Sherborne, 1980

Gibson, Alan and Gibson, Anthony, *West Country Treasury*, Ex Libris Press, Bradford-on-Avon, 1989

Grinsell, L. V., *The Archaeology of Wessex*, Methuen, London, 1958

Hawkins, Desmond, (ed.), *Wessex: A Literary Celebration*, Century, London, 1991

Hyland, Paul, *Purbeck: The Ingrained Island*, Dovecote Press, Wimborne, 1989

Leete, J. A., *Wiltshire Miscellany*, Venton, Melksham, 1976

Legg, Rodney, *Dorset National Trust Guide*, Dorset Publishing, Wincanton, 1992

Literary Dorset, Dorset Publishing, Wincanton, 1990

Purbeck Island, Dorset Publishing, Wincanton, 1972

Leland, John, *The Itinerary of John Leland: Vol. I* (ed. Lucy Toulmin Smith), S. Illinois University, Carbondale, USA, 1964

Long Barrows in Hampshire and the Isle of Wight, H.M.S.O., London, 1979

Malone, Caroline, *Avebury*, Batsford and English Heritage, London, 1989

Massingham, H. J., (ed.), *The Essential Gilbert White of Selborne*, Breslich & Foss, London, 1983

Major, Albany, *Early Wars of Wessex*, Blandford Press, Poole, 1978

Marples, Morris, *White Horses and Other Hill Figures*, Sutton, Stroud, 1981

Mee, Arthur, ed., *Dorset* (Kings of England series), Hodder and Stoughton, London, 1939

Mee, Arthur, ed., *Hampshire with the Isle of Wight* (Kings of England series), Hodder and Stoughton, London, 1939

Morley, Geoffrey, *Smuggling in Hampshire & Dorset 1700-1850*, Countryside Books, Newbury, 1983

Nicolson, Adam, *Wetland Life in the Somerset Levels*, Michael Joseph, London, 1986

Palmer, Kingsley, *Oral Folk-Tales of Wessex*, David & Charles, Newton Abbot, 1973

Palmer, Kingsley, *The Folklore of Somerset*, Batsford, London, 1976

Pevsner, Nikolaus and Newman, John, *Dorset* (The Buildings of England series), Penguin Books, Harmondsworth, 1972

Pevsner, Nikolaus and Lloyd, David, *Hampshire and the Isle of Wight* (The Buildings of England series), Penguin Books, Harmondsworth, 1967

Pevsner, Nikolaus, *North Somerset and Bristol* (The Buildings of England series), Penguin Books, Harmondsworth, 1958

Pevsner, Nikolaus, *South and West Somerset* (The Buildings of England series), Penguin Books, Harmondsworth, 1958

Pevsner, Nikolaus and Cherry, Bridget, *Wiltshire* (The Buildings of England series), Penguin Books, Harmondsworth, 1963

Potter, K. R., (ed.), Gesta Stephani, O.U.P., London, 1976

Small, Donn, and Chapman, John, (ed.), *Explore the New Forest*, H.M.S.O., London, 1987

Steers, J. A., *Coastal Features of England and Wales*, Oleander Press, Cambridge, 1981

Steers, J. A., *The Coastline of England and Wales*, Cambridge University Press, London, 1969

Stukeley, William, *Abury: a Temple of the British Druids with Some Others Described*, London, 1743

Thorn, Caroline and Frank, eds., *Domesday Book: Somerset*, Phillimore, Chichester, 1980

Walker, Frank, *The Bristol Region*, Nelson, London, 1972

Walls, Ernest, *The Bristol Avon*, Arrowsmith, Bristol, 1927

Watts, Kenneth, *The Marlborough Downs*, Ex Libris Press, Bradford-on-Avon, 1993

Whitlock, Ralph, *The Folklore of Wiltshire*, Batsford, London, 1976

Woodforde, James, *Diary of a Country Parson: 1758-1802*, O.U.P., Oxford, 1924-31

Ziegler, Philip, *The Black Death*, Penguin, Harmondsworth, 1969

Index